THE TECH SET

Ellyssa Kroski, Series Editor

Next-Gen Library Redesign

Michael Lascarides

ALA TechSource

An imprint of the American Library Association

Chicago   2012

© 2012 by the American Library Association. Any claim of copyright is subject to applicable limitations and exceptions, such as rights of fair use and library copying pursuant to Sections 107 and 108 of the U.S. Copyright Act. No copyright is claimed for content in the public domain, such as works of the U.S. government.

Printed in the United States of America

Library of Congress Cataloging-in-Publication Data
Lascarides, Michael, 1970–
    Next-gen library redesign / Michael Lascarides.
        p. cm. — (The tech set ; #16)
    Includes bibliographical references and index.
    ISBN 978-1-55570-787-3 (alk. paper)
    1. Libraries—Information technology—Planning. 2. Libraries and the Internet. 3. Library Web sites. 4. Libraries and community. 5. Communication in library administration. I. Title.

Z678.9.L275 2012
020.285'4678—dc23

2012009040

⊚ This paper meets the requirements of ANSI/NISO Z39.48-1992 (Permanence of Paper).

For Mom, who would've gotten a kick out of this

CONTENTS

Don't miss this book's companion website!

Turn the page for details.

THE TECH SET® Volumes 11–20 is more than just the book you're holding!

These 10 titles, along with the 10 titles that preceded them, in THE TECH SET® series feature three components:

1. This book
2. Companion web content that provides more details on the topic and keeps you current
3. Author podcasts that will extend your knowledge and give you insight into the author's experience

The companion webpages and podcasts can be found at:

www.alatechsource.org/techset/

On the website, you'll go far beyond the printed pages you're holding and:

- Access author updates that are packed with new advice and recommended resources
- Use the website comments section to interact, ask questions, and share advice with the authors and your LIS peers
- Hear these pros in screencasts, podcasts, and other videos providing great instruction on getting the most out of the latest library technologies

For more information on THE TECH SET® series and the individual titles, visit **www.neal-schuman.com/techset-11-to-20**.

FOREWORD

Today's next-generation libraries are forces of innovation that are embracing the information revolution brought about through Web 2.0 technology. These cutting-edge libraries are creating engaging experiences for their patrons by incorporating social, open, and mobile functionality into their websites and online catalogs. *Next-Gen Library Redesign* is a one-stop reference manual identifying what it takes to produce a forward-thinking web presence for your library. Author Michael Lascarides delivers invaluable advice and recommendations for incorporating social media into your website, offering collaborative subject guides, highlighting deep collections, and offering mobile catalogs. This outstanding, practical volume guides the reader through the steps necessary to leverage crowdsourcing to create a collection with the help of your patrons, how to promote your librarians through public profiles, and how to establish a unified web presence for your library.

The ten new TECH SET volumes are designed to be even more cutting-edge than the original ten. After the first ten were published and we received such positive feedback from librarians who were using the books to implement technology in their libraries as well as train their staff, it seemed that there would be a need for another TECH SET. And I wanted this next set of books to be even more forward-looking and tackle today's hottest technologies, trends, and practices to help libraries stay on the forefront of technology innovation. Librarians have ceased sitting on the sidelines and have become technology leaders in their own right. This series was created to offer guidance and inspiration to all those aspiring to be library technology leaders themselves.

I originally envisioned a series of books that would offer accessible, practical information that would teach librarians not only how to use new technologies as individuals but also how to plan and implement particular types of library services using them. And when THE TECH SET won the ALA's Greenwood Publishing Group Award for the Best Book in Library Literature, it seemed that we had achieved our goal of becoming the go-to resource for libraries wanting hands-on technology primers. For these new ten books, I thought it was important to incorporate reader feedback by adding two new chapters that would better facilitate learning how to put these new technologies into practice in libraries. The new chapter called "Social Mechanics" discusses strategies for gaining buy-in and support from organizational stakeholders, and the additional "Developing Trends" chapter looks ahead to future directions of these technologies. These new chapters round out the books that discuss the entire life cycle of these tech initiatives, including everything from what it takes to plan, strategize, implement, market, and measure the success of these projects.

While each book covers the A–Zs of each technology being discussed, the hands-on "Implementation" chapters, chock-full of detailed project instructions, account for the largest portions of the books. These chapters start off with a basic "recipe" for how to effectively use the technology in a library and then build on that foundation to offer more and more advanced project ideas. Because these books are designed to appeal to readers of all levels of expertise, both the novice and advanced technologist will find something useful in these chapters, as the proposed projects and initiatives run the gamut from the basic how to create a Foursquare campaign for your library to how to build an iPhone application. Similarly, the new Drupal webmaster will benefit from the instructions for how to configure a basic library website, while the advanced web services librarian may be interested in the instructions for powering a dynamic library website in the cloud using Amazon's EC2 service.

Michael Lascarides has been speaking about and teaching web design and information architecture for many years now and has been keeping the New York Public Library on the cutting edge as their Digital User Analyst. Michael brings his extensive knowledge and expertise to *Next-Gen Library Redesign* in which he guides readers through what it takes to create an innovative web experience today. Extremely well-written and insightful, this is an important resource that every library will want to have in its collection.

Ellyssa Kroski
Manager of Information Systems
New York Law Institute
http://www.ellyssakroski.com/
http://oedb.org/blogs/ilibrarian/
ellyssakroski@yahoo.com

Ellyssa Kroski is the Manager of Information Systems at the New York Law Institute as well as a writer, educator, and international conference speaker. In 2011, she won the ALA's Greenwood Publishing Group Award for the Best Book in Library Literature for THE TECH SET, the ten-book technology series that she created and edited. She's also the author of *Web 2.0 for Librarians and Information Professionals*, a well-reviewed book on web technologies and libraries. She speaks at several conferences a year, mainly about new tech trends, digital strategy, and libraries. She is an adjunct faculty member at Pratt Institute and blogs at *iLibrarian*.

PREFACE

None of the innovations of recent decades have changed the core mission of the library world, which is to both provide access to information for the widest variety of patrons and provide patrons with the tools and guidance to make informed choices with that information. The result of the digital revolution for libraries has been to shift our primary emphasis from the former to the latter; as barriers to access fall, the work of ensuring quality, providing context, and simply making sense of the torrents of information in our patrons' lives becomes paramount.

For this reason, rather than focusing on a single software approach, *Next-Gen Library Redesign* explores numerous web-based technologies, with particular focus on free or low-cost open source software solutions that can be implemented quickly and with little investment. More importantly, it puts those technologies in the context of the larger technological, legal, and social trends emerging from the web and in doing so provides a useful set of tools, heuristics, and guidelines for determining which of those technologies is most worth the investment of your institution's resources. It defines buzzwords and acronyms issuing forth from vendors' press releases to identify the most fundamental new trends in the information landscape and set forth some rules to determine which are the most important for *you*.

Even as a digitally savvy veteran of the first dot-com boom, I often find myself overwhelmed by the sheer quantity of Wonderful New Things with the potential to utterly upend the way libraries do business. From mobile devices to e-books to location-aware services to social networks, it can be difficult just to keep up with the new inventions, let alone distinguish the fads from the game-changers and the new standards. But this new information landscape also presents today's libraries with certain advantages. We can avail ourselves of physical roots in our communities, passionate and loyal patrons, an open community of professional practice that encourages sharing, and our deserved reputation as defenders of a culture of access to information for all.

▶ ORGANIZATION AND AUDIENCE

The introductory chapters of this book give an overview of the "big picture" technology landscape and highlight some of the external forces that are changing the way that the library world works, ways to identify which of those forces are the fundamental ones, and examples of ways that the most agile libraries are adapting to that change.

Chapter 1 highlights the speed at which digital and web technologies are changing the whole of society, not just the library world, and changing the expectations of our patrons about what makes a good digital experience. Chapter 2 gives a broad overview of the variety of (mostly open source and free or low-cost) software available that can be used to quickly and effectively solve some common problems. Chapter 3 lays out tools and techniques to not only follow a project through to completion but also to decide what the highest-priority projects are in the first place for your institution. Chapter 4 discusses how to involve the many stakeholders from across your organization in the process of prioritization and development and how to ensure you get their feedback. Chapter 5 offers six sample projects to break down the barriers between your online patrons and your collections, beginning with an inventory and "spring cleaning" of all of your web properties, moving through simple ways to encourage sharing and discovery, and moving on to more sophisticated ways of actually collaborating with your patrons to create new content. Chapter 6 highlights how to let both your patrons and your staff know about the new projects you've launched and how to sustain them, and it offers strategies for "learning by doing" in using the new projects themselves as marketing tools. Chapter 7 describes ways of using digital technologies to build communities, lower your workload, and maximize the number of ways that your patrons can connect to your institution and your collections. Chapter 8 lays out a comprehensive plan for undertaking the all-important task of determining just how much your efforts are making an impact, incorporating qualitative and quantitative techniques from both traditional and next-generation sources. Chapter 9 looks at just a few of the new technologies on the horizon both within and without the library world with the potential to reshape our world once again.

If you are a librarian with basic to intermediate web technology skills, *Next-Gen Library Redesign* can help you make sense of what's behind the urgency of the new web-based technologies being implemented by today's forward-thinking libraries. And if you're a more advanced technologist, this book will teach tips and techniques that you can apply to your practice to make sure that the services that you're already providing are coherent, sensible, and useful.

I hope that you'll be able to use the projects contained in *Next-Gen Library Redesign* at your own institution to create the best possible experiences for your patrons. But beyond the software projects, I hope that the practical insights this book offers can help you calmly and critically evaluate and navigate the immense changes that digital, networked, and mobile technologies are imposing on our libraries and turn them from a source of stress into a source of innovation, creativity, and success.

▶1

INTRODUCTION

▶ **Disruptive Innovation**
▶ **It's All about the Experience**

Way back in that earlier age of technology known as mid-2007, if you wanted to purchase a small, easy-to-use electronic device dedicated to reading books in electronic format, your choices were decidedly limited. A number of earlier devices (such as the Rocket eBook) had come and gone, burdened by dark, low-contrast LCD screens, bulky batteries, small memory capacity, and awkward usability. The *Wikipedia* page surveying e-book readers listed only six products.

Had you been listening to conversations within libraries about e-books at that time, you would have heard a lot of optimism for the e-book format, tempered by a healthy dose of skepticism. Libraries had long been intrigued about delivering texts to their patrons electronically because the advantages were many: digital copies are cheap, can be delivered on demand, and can be created on the fly, mitigating the need for extensive planning from the collections development staff.

But arguments were also being made that e-books might never live up to the hype. After all, we *knew* certain things. E-books are difficult to use. E-book readers strain the eyes far more than paper books. Our patrons don't read long-form works on the screen. Nobody owns these dedicated devices, and it's expensive for us to buy enough of them. And our patrons tell us they just like paper better.

In November 2007, online retailer Amazon announced that it would start selling its own e-book reader, called the Kindle. The Kindle represented a great leap forward in getting usable e-book technology into the hands (quite literally) of a mass audience for the first time. It was a lightweight, simple device that fit easily into a bag or coat pocket. It had a simple, intuitive interface, with dedicated buttons to flip pages and scroll up and down through a document. Memory was solid-state and abundant, meaning the device could hold immense amounts of text and images without fragile hard drives.

Amazon made it easy to load new e-books onto the device, even allowing customers to purchase new titles from the device itself. And the Kindle used a high-resolution "E-ink" display that, unlike typical back-lit computer screens, mimicked the appearance of paper.

The device, while far from perfect, wiped out a large chunk of the criticism against earlier e-book readers the day it launched. It was easy to use, it fit nicely in the hand, and it was no more or less hard to read than a trade paperback. And this time, it was backed by the biggest book retailer in the industry.

It is estimated that by mid-2010, with the Kindle already in its third generation, more than four million of them had been sold (Wilhelm, 2010). Backed by deals with major publishers and deeply integrated into Amazon's own groundbreaking e-commerce system, it single-handedly created the first mass market for e-books.

For libraries, the question about e-books quickly shifted from "When?" to "What about us?" The Kindle platform was relatively closed, making interoperability with existing e-book distribution systems difficult. There were questions about its copy-protection software and distribution rights. But no one was asking when will e-books hit the mainstream anymore.

Another big leap in e-book reader technology was Apple's introduction of the iPad, a touch screen tablet computer, in early 2010. A video was posted on YouTube (YouTube, 2010) a day or two after the first iPads were delivered to customers, and it has been viewed more than one million times. In it, a father (just off camera) hands his new iPad to his two-and-a-half-year-old daughter, bright eyed and adorable in her butterfly-print pajamas. Despite having never seen the iPad before, the little girl starts swiping through the choices, pressing buttons, and launching and closing applications within ten seconds. When a barely verbal child can deduce the basic operations of a computer (and despite the form factor and reduced interface, it most certainly is a computer) almost instantly, we are clearly dealing with a new kind of interactive experience.

The lesson for libraries about the Kindle and iPad is that it takes only one or two seminal products to turn "might happen someday" into "we have to do this now." A banner ad on Amazon's homepage, or the words "...and it will be in stores tomorrow!" from a grinning, be-turtlenecked Steve Jobs, and suddenly that future is here.

▶ DISRUPTIVE INNOVATION

E-book readers (and, more significantly, their attendant online bookstores) are just one innovation with the potential to impact the core business of libraries. There are dozens of them, starting with the World Wide Web itself and including search engines, social networks, e-books, e-commerce, smartphones, *Wikipedia*, Google Books, recommendation and rating sites, location-aware networks, QR codes, digital television, online video, podcasting, blogging—the list can seem endless.

But the library world is by no means alone, as dozens of industries are struggling with the creative disruption wrought by a super-empowered, networked audience. The music and film industries find themselves in pitched battles against illegal downloads of their copyrighted materials and the increased competition afforded by lower production costs. Universities see potential threats in low-cost, online instruction. Newspapers seem to be fighting battles on every front, from social networks' ability to instantaneously spread stories, depriving them of scoops, to the global competition now one click away, to the high cost of printing thousands of paper copies daily, to the loss of revenue from classified ads supplanted by the likes of Craigslist. Magazines, television, academic journals, advertising—a vast segment of the global economy is coping with what economist Clayton Christensen (2003) has termed "disruptive innovation." Christensen spent years studying why some businesses thrive and others die in the face of changing circumstances. His work describes how even well-managed companies that are responsive to their customers' needs can find themselves outperformed by others offering inferior products. Specifically, he examines how the markets for particular products behave when new competitors arise, making a distinction between "low-end disruption," where innovators target an audience that doesn't need the full value of the best product in the market, and "new-market disruption," where the new players find new markets that were unserved (or underserved) by existing products.

For libraries, the implication of the theory of disruptive innovation is that neither providing high-quality content nor offering free access will, by themselves, save us. Let's assume for a moment that libraries are an industry, offering a product (access to all kinds of information) to customers (our patrons) and arrayed against a host of innovative competitors. In Christensen's (2003) model, we are the incumbent supplier. There are many forms of information for which libraries had previously been the exclusive supplier, but now we compete against others on the web who offer a qualitatively inferior but easily procured product. Google and *Wikipedia* now compete with the reference librarian. Tax forms and government data are supplied by the agencies themselves on their own websites. Enough academic journals and peer-reviewed materials are freely available to offer a good start on most research projects. The list goes on.

Librarians take justifiable pride in the quality and value of the information products they produce and are passionate defenders of long-form text in print, deep collections, and original sources. Google, we assure our patrons, doesn't contain even remotely close to everything. Yet the history of commerce is littered with the wreckage of innovative companies that made products that were far superior to those of their competitors. The important question isn't "Do libraries have better content?" but "Can our patrons get a 'good enough' version of what we offer somewhere else?" Where the answer to this last question is "yes," we need to act. And fast.

Another defense of libraries is that we give away that better product for free. However, much content on the web is free, as well. Our patrons are practically swimming in no-cost content, both within and without the library.

Libraries may offer cheaper and higher-quality resources than our other sources, but we're not necessarily easier to use. If we cost our patrons time, aggravation, and effort, they will certainly look around for less-stressful options. And there's more bad news: it's not just free against free. Precedents show that often people would rather *pay* for a good experience than endure a bad one for free.

As an example, look to Apple's launch of the iTunes Music Store in 2003. At the time of its launch, the illegal file-sharing service Napster had already come and gone and peer-to-peer file sharing was on the rise. Apple proceeded anyway with its new online music store, getting buy-in from a number of large recording labels and building software that placed a premium on usability (something that earlier, now-forgotten competitors had been criticized as lacking). Apple saw that free, ubiquitous, and illegal downloads *didn't actually offer a great alternative*. They could be hit-or-miss to find, were often mislabeled, and were wildly varying in quality. The software to access them was usually difficult to configure and use. And, of course, they were still illegal.

The Music Store was an instant success. By 2010, Apple had sold ten billion songs, most at 99 cents each (Apple Corporation, 2010). That's roughly ten billion dollars made selling something that any smart teenager (with a willingness to bend the rules) could grab from the Internet without paying. Drawn by a simple, consistent interface, good selection, and excellent quality control, people became iTunes customers because buying music from iTunes was a better experience than the free alternative. Sometimes, you get what you pay for.

► IT'S ALL ABOUT THE EXPERIENCE

For this reason, libraries must pay attention to what other media and information innovators are offering to our patrons when they're not at the library. Google, Facebook, Netflix, Twitter, Amazon, Apple, *The New York Times*, and others set the standard for what good, useful interactive experiences *feel* like, not just what they offer. Every new innovation in user experience they roll out raises the library patron's expectations of what is possible—and expected.

Make no mistake: free access and compelling content are immeasurably valuable resources. But without partnering those two with engaging, easy-to-use experiences, libraries run the risk of dissatisfaction, dwindling audiences, and disuse. Fortunately, the barriers to entry for creating great software have lowered immensely in recent years and are even within the grasp of libraries with limited technical staff.

And libraries possess a number of advantages over other online sources of media and information. Our buildings and our history of face-to-face interactions give us deep, physical roots in our communities; when so much socializing happens through a glowing screen, places to meet and converse in the real world take on added value. Libraries have an open community of professional practice that encourages sharing, even between "rival" institutions. And libraries have a deserved reputation as impartial defenders of a culture of access to information for all and as an important counterbalance against excessive corporate influence or government regulation.

In the short term, it is the loyalty of our patrons that is perhaps the most important of advantages. A recent survey in the United Kingdom found that 74 percent of library users and 59 percent of nonusers considered that nation's libraries to perform an "important" or "essential" role in their communities (Sharma, 2010). That's an audience that will gladly pitch in and help us evolve with the changing media landscape. Beneath the numbers, the connection with the library goes beyond mere satisfaction and into something that looks a lot like love. Love of books, love of reading, love of learning, love of discovery—these *emotional* connections power the library of today.

However, today's loyalty is borne of the decades of previously invested good experiences delivered to an audience that had far fewer media and reading choices. For the library of the future to have as passionate an audience in decades to come, we need to ensure that we're offering interactive and discovery experiences that are as good as the offerings they are becoming used to outside the library. The 2008 U.S. election included the first voters who have never taken a breath in a world without the web. Right behind them, the so-called "Millennial Generation" and "Digital Natives" (like that two-and-a-half-year-old with her father's iPad) are much more comfortable in a media-saturated world and will demand a higher quality of tools. Those kids *are* that "next generation" for whom we need to create the perfect library.

So, what exactly *is* a next-generation library? I offer that being a next-generation library is about taking a certain attitude toward the future, one that sees in the increasing rate of technological and social change not a threat to what we've done before but an opportunity for what we can do now. A next-generation library:

- embraces the technology that's the best tool for the job and has the nerve to stick with traditional methods where they are best;
- moves from a service model of "face-to-face" to one of "shoulder-to-shoulder" and acts as a guide, not as a gatekeeper (Underhill, 2000);
- doesn't see the digital and the physical as distinct, circumscribed modes but instead embraces them as deeply complementary and overlapping;
- listens to patrons and uses every possible communication tool to engage them in two-way conversations;
- uses technology of all kinds to improve discoverability of and access to collections as radically and broadly as possible; and
- doesn't get upset when patrons go somewhere else for information but adjusts to and learns from the new information landscape (in other words, don't fight Google or *Wikipedia*—participate in them!).

A "next-generation library," then, is not an official appellation. It's not dependent on having a huge staff. There's no qualifying test or club membership awarded, no gold plaque from a governing body you can affix to your front entrance. "Next-generation-ness" is, at core, no more or less than *an attitude toward change.*

The accelerating rate of technological and societal change can be seen as threatening or frustrating, but it instills librarians with a sense of purpose, on two fronts. First, by learning to embrace change, we can constantly reevaluate and improve our services and offerings; and second, we can offer our patrons an unbiased, guided journey through *their* relationship with this new change. Privacy, copyright, search engines, new technologies, sharing, piracy, new formats, new devices—when even the most tech-savvy among us finds it exhausting to keep up, imagine the plight of the average, not-so-tech-savvy patron trying to make sense of all of it.

It's become a bit of a cliché to say that the only thing you can be sure of is change, but the past four decades or so have made it clear that our communications and information technologies have exceeded all but the wildest science fiction. If it seems *possible* that some new digital technology Thing might be available on the Internet in a couple of years, then the smart money is on someone building a prototype, someone else making it usable, and a third someone making it ubiquitous.

Faced with such barbaric interlopers, the traditional library of popular culture (you know all the staid and old-fashioned caricatures, I'm sure) bars the door, barricades the stacks, and launches into a passionate defense of the beauty of paper. But the next-generation library, with grace, agility, and faith in the ability of print to easily endure alongside the digital, accepts innovation as inevitable, finds the newcomers a place to sit, and puts them to work making patrons happy.

In this book, we will look at ways that modern libraries are embracing change and offer practical, hands-on tutorials to implement those changes yourself. But readers should think about their own institutions and look for ways to move beyond the installation of software and into a critique of all of the barriers preventing you from giving your patrons better experiences. It takes innovation and evolution on the legal, management, and partnership fronts as much as the financial or technical to equip your library to be comfortable with change.

Let's get started.

▶ 2

TYPES OF SOLUTIONS AVAILABLE

▶ **Choose the Right Software Model for Your Library**

▶ **Explore Your Options**

▶CHOOSE THE RIGHT SOFTWARE MODEL FOR YOUR LIBRARY

Using technology to change your library's relationship to its staff and patrons inevitably means new software. You have a number of options available to you, ranging from off-the-shelf, free web-based applications (which may be cheap and easy but not very customizable) to contracting with a software vendor to build you a custom solution from scratch (complicated and expensive but exactly tailored to your needs), with every variation in between. Here's a nonexhaustive list of questions that can help you understand the kind of software solution that's the best fit for your organization.

▶ Do you have technical staff available to you? Are you even capable of customizing software?

▶ Is your budget fixed or variable? What is the lead time for getting new expenditures approved?

▶ How large is your technical team? What are their skill sets? All technical skills are not created equal. Some developers are whizzes at getting databases to run but are at a loss when it comes to fixing the layout of a website, while others can make beautiful templates but don't know how to import data. If you build a web application in one language, will there be others on your staff who can work on it?

▶ Do you have access to permanent programmers or only to freelancers? If you're at an academic library, are the programmers developing your applications graduate students? Will they be around in two years to do the maintenance when the system needs an upgrade, or will they have graduated? Is there a plan in place to transition if they do?

▶ Do you have an external technical services team? Do they have limitations on the kinds of software they support? Do they have a process for purchasing software systems?

▶ How is software paid for in your organization? Are you better off with a large, one-time capital cost or with costs spread out over a number of years as a subscription service?

▶ EXPLORE YOUR OPTIONS

Open Source Software

One of the most important trends in software in the past two decades has been the emergence of free and open source software into the corporate and institutional mainstream. Open source projects, typically built by individuals or small groups and then released in full to the public with very open, often explicitly noncommercial licenses, have proven to be just as robust in many instances as their commercial counterparts.

Given its openness and focus on support by a globally networked community, open source software makes a very sensible match for libraries in many cases. The advantages of open source software include the following:

▶ **Low initial cost:** With no/very low subscription or license fees, getting your hands on the software is as easy as downloading a copy.

▶ **Customizability:** Any programmer has access to any of the code, so any needed modifications are fair game.

▶ **Standards compliance and interoperability:** Given that most open source software development is anathema to proprietary commercial standards, its products tend to adhere much more closely to published standards.

▶ **Community:** User communities are built around most of the larger open source software projects.

There are, of course, corresponding drawbacks to these positives:

▶ **Complexity:** While it sounds compelling to download an application and go, open source tools are not always built around ease of installation given that their target audience is often of a hacker-ish bent.

▶ **Ongoing support:** Even in cases where open source products may be easy to set up, libraries with limited technical resources may prefer to have a company on the other end of the line to whom they can reach out when something goes wrong.

▶ **Documentation:** Frequently, although the quality of coding can be very high (even exceeding their commercial counterparts), the written help and documentation around open source projects can be pretty grim for the less-technical user.

Despite these drawbacks, open source tools have become critical to the operation of all sorts of organizations from corporations to government to museums to libraries. A recommended approach is to download, install, and customize your own software initially but to work with one of the many companies springing up to offer ongoing and emergency support of your applications. See the companion website (http://www.alatechsource.org/ techset/) for more information about companies offering open source software support.

Wikis

Wikis have been around for a while now and are familiar to most people. They are an excellent tool for posting content while offering maximum flexibility of editing and an extremely low barrier to participation. The guiding principle of a wiki is that anyone should be able to edit any of its pages at any time. The ultimate expression of "wiki-ness" is, of course, *Wikipedia*, whose "anything goes" ethos belies the fact that its army of volunteers has banded together to enforce strong community standards. Wiki software is also varied, abundant, and usually free. To create your own, there are a number of choices available. Your first choice is whether to install your own software or use a hosted service.

On hosted services such as Wikispaces.com, Wikispot.org, or Google's Google Sites, you can simply create an account (usually for free or for a very low monthly fee, depending on the options you desire), and start using your wiki there. Any users wishing to contribute then would create an account on that service's domain. Bear in mind that because these sites are third-party hosted, additional terms and conditions regarding registration, privacy, and ownership of content may apply. Make sure to read the fine print! While the advantage of a hosted service is little to no setup, the disadvantage is that you lack control over all aspects. Make sure that the hosted wiki you choose has policies that match those of your library; you don't want to encourage contributors to sign up using their e-mail address or other personal information on a service with which you aren't completely comfortable.

The other wiki option is to install your own software. Your own wiki has the advantage of complete control and accordance with your library policies but the disadvantage of a bit more work to set up the software initially. If you're uncomfortable with setting up your own software on a web server, many web hosting companies these days offer one-click installs of popular open source software packages, which usually includes a wiki package or two. You can purchase a hosted account for $5–$10 a month, click to install the wiki software, enter some basic configuration information, and be ready to begin within 20–30 minutes.

Popular wiki packages include MediaWiki (renowned for being the platform that powers *Wikipedia*), Confluence (a Java-based platform used mainly in corporate and software development environments), and TWiki (a Perl-based application with strong collaboration tools). If you're unsure about which is right for you, MediaWiki is a popular, safe choice, and it has the added bonus of sharing code with *Wikipedia*; any of your contributors who have edited *Wikipedia* will feel right at home.

Content Management Software

Many of the popular open source content management systems (CMS) popular with libraries, such as Drupal or Joomla, come with a certain amount of infrastructure out of the box, such as user accounts, editing screens, and the ability to create relationships between different types of content.

They are not designed from the outset as collaborative editing tools, so, unlike wiki software, they will not allow multiple users to directly edit existing content at the same time. However, they do enable you to quickly create new, precisely defined content types. Depending on how you have framed your project, you can use these defined content types to your advantage. For example, if part of your work is to catalog the characteristics of a number of collections within your library, you can create a "collection" content type with its own required fields and built-in validations.

In software design, fewer options are usually better for usability than too many, and while it may seem intuitive that more features would be better, in practice this is rarely the case. One of the drawbacks of the wiki approach is too much freedom. Where the free-form text entry style of content building used by wikis would certainly allow you to create a list of collections, a CMS, by virtue of knowing more about its structure, would also allow that list of collections to be sorted, filtered, repurposed, and easily pulled into other forms of presentation—other webpages, downloadable delimited data files, or semantic markup for an application programming interface (API).

If you're using a CMS to manage information on your library website, you can automatically relate items to each other: subject guides, blog posts, event listings, finding aids, maps to physical locations, and so forth. These connections mean that, for example, a description of a genealogy collection in the subject guide can be related to a previously written blog post about genealogy, after which a link to the blog post can automatically appear on the appropriate part of the subject guide, and a link to the subject guide can appear on the blog post. The creator of the subject guide creates the relationship, and the display happens automatically.

Drupal is one of the CMSs that manages this kind of content relationship natively. For more on getting the most out of Drupal for your library, see *Drupal in Libraries* by Kenneth J. Varnum (THE TECH SET #14).

Blogs

As blogging has matured, solutions for incorporating blogs into your site have become both more abundant and more specialized. Some of the more sophisticated options approach the content management platforms in the richness of their features, just as Drupal and other CMSs have powerful blogging features. WordPress, to name one, is a very popular blogging platform notable for its ease of use and customization options, offering a wide variety of optional plug-ins to handle different types of media. It is available as a hosted service or downloadable software you can install on your own server.

Blogger is Google's free online blogging software. A bit less flexible and extensible than WordPress, it has the advantage of simplicity and ease of use, and it can be used to power a website running under your own domain name. As of this writing, some technology media outlets were reporting that Google intends to retire the Blogger brand and roll it into Google+, the company's new social network, so the landscape may have changed by the time you read this (Parr, 2011).

Tumblr, which is a very visually oriented type of blogging service built around the sharing of images, is another offering that straddles the line between blogging platform and social network. While Flickr or another photo-sharing site is better for organizing groups of images, Tumblr is great for "picture of the day"-type applications in an environment that encourages sharing.

There are dozens of other viable blogging platforms. See this book's companion website (http://www.alatechsource.org/techset/) for a more detailed list.

Using Social Media Platforms for Content Management

If your project revolves around the creation of images, audio, or video, another low-cost, low-effort way of getting participation from your patrons is to make use of social media platforms like Flickr or YouTube. Looking to build a community-curated exhibition? Encourage patrons to upload their own images and "tag" them with a particular unique tag on these sites. For example, as part of a recent exhibition about religion here at the New York Public Library, we encouraged patrons to upload their own images about what faith meant to them and tag those images with the unique phrase "faith on the street." We then used a search for that special tag to gather posted images and create a gallery on our exhibition website. (This approach is excellent for gathering images or video on a particular topic from the patrons themselves.) See "Incorporate Social Media into Your Website" in Chapter 5 for a detailed look at the features of the different types of social media platforms available.

LibGuides

If your goal is simply to have a very good framework for the staff to post content in a library-centric tool, you might want to take a look at a widely used commercial web application called LibGuides (http://www.springshare .com/libguides/) from Springshare. LibGuides is a hosted web service (no software installation necessary) with a wide variety of features, including easily embedding audio and video materials, formatting for easy readability on mobile devices, integrating with chat, social networks, and e-mail, and an API for adding and repurposing LibGuides content onto your other websites. At the time of this writing, the subscription costs for the LibGuides service run between a few hundred to a few thousand dollars a year (Springshare, 2011), depending on the size of your library, but check with the vendor for current pricing.

LibGuides is not a wiki-like collaborative creation tool but is more about adding lots of linked content in many formats and managing your guides among your staff. It also allows you to respond quickly to feedback from your patrons.

Mobile Solutions

Most major OPAC (online public access catalog) vendors offer some form of mobile access, either as an option or as part of their core offerings. Before going any further with development, check with your library's OPAC vendor to see if you already have access to an app or mobile website. For example, both SirsiDynix and Innovative Interfaces, two of the largest OPAC vendors, offer mobile web versions of their catalogs and have started to experiment with apps.

The California-based company Boopsie offers an intriguing solution for libraries wishing to broadly support mobile technology. Its subscription-based service requires the setup of a point of integration with your library's OPAC, after which Boopsie builds a number of applications for your library, with versions for each major mobile platform (iOS, Android, mobile web, Black-Berry, etc.). Its applications can be integrated with most of the major OPAC platforms, and, in addition to an interesting "as-you-type" search interface, it supplies a GPS-aware library locator, an "Ask a Librarian" feature, reading lists, and calendars of events.

The library services platform BiblioCommons also offers a mobile version of their shared, social catalog interface, with a mobile website as well as apps for iPhone and Android. These apps are extensions of the BiblioCommons platform and therefore are available only to those libraries that are using it. However, for BiblioCommons users, the apps are a very low-effort option to implement.

Finally, if you are developing your own mobile solutions, any webpage can be made more mobile friendly with a style sheet that specifically controls its display on mobile devices. Such style sheets can be brought into the page with either standard cascading style sheet rules or more sophisticated client- or server-side detection techniques.

Like many of the specific software products mentioned in this book, the mobile library catalog application field is an area of intense innovation and rapid change. You would be well-served to seek out any new products before choosing a software solution. Check the companion website (http://www .alatechsource.org/techset/) for an updated list of available mobile software. The wiki page of resources and links from the annual M-Libraries conference on mobile technology in libraries (http://www.libsuccess.org/index.php? title=M-Libraries) is also a great, frequently updated resource to keep up with new releases. For instructions on how to build your own mobile website and applications, see Jason A. Clark's *Building Mobile Library Applications* (THE TECH SET #12).

Custom Software Development

If you have a task for which there is not an available tool and you have access to programming resources, coding your own software can be an attractive option. Keep in mind, however, that much of the lifetime cost of a piece of custom software is in the maintenance and upgrades that happen after the application is written.

Even if you choose to go the more difficult custom-coding route, it is worth a look around to see if there are any similar projects from which you might be able to borrow. The library, museum, and archives communities tend to be fairly generous with their ideas, and many successful projects have been ultimately released as free and/or open source code. Popular web-development languages like PHP, Python, and Ruby have large, active communities of developers, and projects written in these languages can become mini-communities in their own right composed of like-minded developers who are working for similar institutions and solving common problems. Downloading an existing project that's similar to yours and modifying it can gain you the advantages of custom coding (a software application that's tailored to solve exactly your problem) without having to start completely from scratch. Plus, it may turn out that your modifications can become a contribution to the open project, making it easier for the next person who comes along looking to set up their own project similar to yours.

▶ 3

PLANNING

- ▶ **Understand the Problem You Are Trying to Solve**
- ▶ **Know Your Schedule**
- ▶ **Put Tools in Place for Tracking Time**
- ▶ **Implement Faceted Feature Analysis**
- ▶ **Determine Impact and Return on Investment**

While it can seem to be an incredibly daunting task to get started on a technology project, it needn't be intimidating. Take the time to read this book through completely and choose the projects that seem most within your grasp. Make decisions about which moves will bring the greatest return on your investment of time, money, and resources; it may turn out that a smaller project will have the most impact for you. This chapter will present some tools for defining your problem as much as possible before proceeding.

▶ UNDERSTAND THE PROBLEM YOU ARE TRYING TO SOLVE

When starting a project of any complexity, little is more fundamental than having a firm understanding of the problem you are trying to solve. A simple one-page "mission statement" that can be posted in a shared document or distributed to your team will serve as an important focal point to keep the project on track. Note that it should not confuse the problem you need to solve with its solution. If you need a new library website, the problem is not "build a new website"; rather, the problem is, "our current website does not adequately serve our patrons because it is too hard for them to find the most commonly sought items." See "Create a Unified Library Web Presence" in Chapter 5 for detailed information about creating an inventory of your websites and resources, an exercise that will go a long way toward revealing the "problems" requiring solutions.

▶ KNOW YOUR SCHEDULE

The time that it takes to launch a project varies wildly, and depends on a number of variables including:

- ▶ your available budget;
- ▶ your available staff;
- ▶ technical issues, including software obsolescence, the expiration of support contracts, and growth in traffic, that strain aging systems;
- ▶ the quality of the product you want to deliver;
- ▶ the number of features you want to include;
- ▶ external limitations, such as committed grant schedules, dependencies to/from other projects, and the academic calendar; and
- ▶ the time expectations of your management and your patrons.

Of these factors, the last one often seems far more important than it is. Of course your bosses and your patrons will want great tools (and want them yesterday), but, given that the nature of the relationship between most libraries and their patrons is a loyal, ongoing one and that time, budget, and product quality work in tension with each other, there's often a very compelling reason to ask them to wait.

These days, libraries are frequently working with limited or fixed project budgets, leaving delivery time and the quality of product as the variables in project planning. Do everything you can to keep the quality of the final product as high as possible (i.e., creating a satisfying experience for the end users). This means working on setting expectations with patrons and management. In a business where we are sustained by the goodwill of our patrons, it's better to deliver a great experience next month than a bad experience today.

▶ PUT TOOLS IN PLACE FOR TRACKING TIME

The success of a web project is not determined solely by the quality of the software and the happiness of the patrons; you must also factor in the amount of your limited resources that were required to complete the job. When the project is completed, it will be helpful to look back and see precisely where your team spent their time. As such, it's important to establish a system for tracking time spent on different tasks.

There are a number of terrific web-based time-tracking applications, such as Harvest (http://www.getharvest.com/), that will allow you and your staff to easily keep track of the tasks they worked on. This software (and others like it—see this book's companion website at http://www.alatechsource.org/

techset/ for more links) is very easy to use but allows flexibility in project task tracking and reporting. Pricing varies depending on the size of the team and the number of projects, but it is very reasonable and comes with a free trial. If you are working with an outside vendor, you can simply require it to keep track of the time spent as a condition of its hiring and report it to you at the delivery of the project.

▶ IMPLEMENT FACETED FEATURE ANALYSIS

Starting a new web project can be daunting. Beyond the technical challenges, there's the difficulty in getting all of your stakeholders to agree on a prioritized list of features to include. When everyone wants to contribute their ideas, the outcome can be a mess.

The Faceted Feature Analysis (FFA) is a relatively simple and low-cost spreadsheet-based technique for getting consensus around which features to pursue with limited resources. First proposed in a 2007 article by Adam Polansky (2007) on the web development blog *Boxes and Arrows*, the FFA commences with a list of features. This is a good group exercise at the beginning of a project, where every feature—from "must-dos" to the completely preposterous—are listed in a single column, comprising a complete list of everything your team has considered implementing. For best results, make the features as granular as possible (i.e., avoid generalities like "Start a blog"; instead, list individual, detailed features like "Allow staff to publish blog posts on topics," "Allow users to post comments," and "Allow anonymous commenting"). Don't worry about the practicality of the ideas, as any impractical ideas should perform rather poorly in the ranking steps to come.

The second part of the FFA is to assign a score to each feature in three different categories: Value to the User, Value to the Business Owner, and Technical Feasibility (see Figure 3.1). These three categories should be familiar to anyone who's ever taken a systems analysis or project management class. (A professor of mine summarized it as, "Fast, cheap, and good: pick two.") Scores range from 1 to 10. Once scores fill each column, the columns themselves are weighted 3×, 2×, or 1×, depending on which column you deem most important. If you're operating on a tight budget with limited technical staff, your weighting might go Business, Technical, then User. But if you have on-staff programmers with free time and a willingness to experiment, you might weight User first, then Business, then Technical.

Once the scores and weights are added, you can sort by the composite score, and the things at the top of the list should be the most critically important and easy to accomplish. It's not infallible, but it makes an excellent centerpiece to the conversation about what to build and brings a measure of objective rigor

▶ Figure 3.1: A Faceted Feature Analysis Worksheet

	A	B	C	D	AD
1	feature	tech complexity	business value	user value	Weighted results
2	Hours input/output; for main hours pages plus individual branch/research pages	8.80	10.00	9.33	55.1
3	Admin Interface Allows create/modify/delete of hours	8.80	9.33	8.69	53.1
4	Admin Interface Allows create/modify/delete of locations	8.80	9.33	8.62	53.0
5	Physical Locations: Computers for public use	8.60	9.25	8.92	52.9
6	Physical Locations: Wheelchair accessibility	8.60	9.25	8.92	52.9
7	Physical Locations: Wireless access	8.60	9.25	8.67	52.4
8	Physical Locations: Assistive technologies available	8.60	9.25	8.50	52.1
9	Travel directions input/output on individual branch/research locations	8.60	9.25	8.46	52.0
10	Associate blog posts with user profiles	8.60	8.25	8.91	51.9
11	Admin Interface Allows create/modify/delete of travel directions	8.80	8.33	8.38	51.5
12	Timestamp	9.20	7.50	7.92	50.9
13	Subjects are assigned to Research Guides, subscription databases, Best of the Web, Digital Gallery and items in the library catalogs	8.00	9.50	8.58	50.7
14	Attribute input/output; things like address, phone number, email, accessibility icon status, staff contact	8.40	9.00	8.20	50.6
15	Blog post stream	8.40	8.50	8.33	50.4
16	Author byline linked to user profile	8.60	7.75	8.40	50.4

to an otherwise fraught process. I encourage you to read more about the details of the FFA process on the companion website (http://www.alatechsource .org/techset/), where you will also find a blank FFA spreadsheet template.

▶ DETERMINE IMPACT AND RETURN ON INVESTMENT

In the business world, a company's bottom-line success is measured by its profit, that is, the amount left over when expenses are removed from income. If a business brings in more money than it spends, it is said to be profitable. Those within a business who have an interest in maximizing profit look at the return on investment (ROI) of its various components. With the goal of maximizing profit, companies break down their departments, product lines, and special projects into smaller pieces and analyze their impact in relation to one another.

The library world, however, does not have a profit-maximizing structure. When a library is in the "business" of giving away content for free, it can be difficult even to see the bottom line, let alone determine the ROI of different divisions within a library. Still, understanding how much benefit for the end user has been acquired for each dollar or staff hour spent is the key to determining if a project has been a success or failure.

In a circulating public library, quantitative metrics to measure abound, many of which can be used as proxies for success. It can be helpful if one thinks about the circulation business as a "successful transaction" rather than a "sale." By this measure, there are many opportunities to measure successful transactions:

- Physical visitors coming in the door
- Unique visitors to the website
- Total visits to the website
- Reference interactions (questions answered, etc.)
- Materials circulated or requested
- Searches for materials on the website/catalog resulting in a request for materials
- New library cards and/or accounts created
- Mailing list/social media sign-ups
- Attendance at library events

At a major research library, assessment of impact gets a lot harder, because generally the cost of serving the kinds of materials that are valuable to researchers is much higher than that of a public library and the outcome of that research is much more sophisticated, varied, and subtle. Two reports put out by the Association of College and Research Libraries (Tenopir et al., 2010; Kingma, 2010) are excellent sources for deeper reading on the topic of research library assessment.

Given the immense number of variables that have an impact on any modern library of any size—location, demographics, public or academic, uniqueness of holdings, number of competitors—the more you can learn about measuring them, the better off you will be. See Chapter 7, "Best Practices," for more on identifying and marketing to new audiences you aren't currently reaching and Chapter 8, "Metrics," for an in-depth discussion about how to track the value of your library's transactions.

▶4

SOCIAL MECHANICS

- ▶ **Listen to Your Patrons**
- ▶ **Elicit Feedback from Your Librarians**
- ▶ **Seek Out Your Phone Librarians**
- ▶ **Consult with Your Information Technology/Systems Personnel**
- ▶ **Consult with Your Legal Experts**
- ▶ **Get Management Support**
- ▶ **Provide Appropriate Staff Training**
- ▶ **Choose the Right Software Vendor**

The projects in this book touch every aspect of a library's digital presence. Some require communication skills, some require technical savvy, some require money. All of them affect the public you serve. It helps to understand at the outset how you will need to coordinate others inside and outside of your organization.

▶ LISTEN TO YOUR PATRONS

Ultimately, the success or failure of any systems redesign is going to depend on whether or not it adds value for your patrons. As such, they are the most important stakeholders in any project now and always. Communication with your patrons is imperative and should start with listening.

Every organization is unique, and a large part of what makes your organization unique is your patrons. Just because other organizations similar to your own are implementing certain features and new services successfully doesn't mean that those same features and services will be successful for you. Before you launch into any major upgrade process, a round of listening to your patrons is an absolute necessity. You may find that the latest, greatest Web 2.0 social sharing feature that looks excessively cool on the page is not at all what your patrons are looking for.

Solicit patron feedback at every step of the process. During the planning phase, read any direct suggestions offered by patrons from your physical suggestion box or online suggestion form. Respond if possible; if you have too much feedback to respond to individually, let the patrons know right up front that they will not be receiving a response so they do not wait in vain.

Patrons should also be alerted when changes are approaching. Whenever possible, offer beta periods and public previews of any new software tools so patrons have a chance to acclimate, experiment, and offer feedback. Sudden, abrupt changes without warning can throw people off. See Chapter 8, "Metrics," for more on methodology for learning about your patrons' needs.

▶ ELICIT FEEDBACK FROM YOUR LIBRARIANS

Your librarians are second only in importance to your patrons in the hierarchy of those who matter, because they deal with patrons all day long. They will have an immediate, intimate knowledge of "pain points" within the organization, because, when current systems are not fulfilling patron needs, patrons will turn to librarians for help.

Librarians are of course not only conduits of knowledge about the habits of patrons, but are themselves important users of any new web technologies. They will be your first beta testers and most important source of feedback.

That said, be aware that although librarians possess hugely important and vital information about how the library is used on a day-to-day basis, their knowledge is largely anecdotal in nature. Librarians can be biased because they hear from those who are having trouble or struggling, which may mask an indeterminate number of patrons succeeding at the same task. Librarians are also notorious for being experts in their own jargon and may recommend labels and instructions that make sense to librarians but not to the general public. For maximum impact, the extraordinarily valuable anecdotal insights of librarians are best balanced with quantitative metrics and constructive qualitative feedback from patrons.

▶ SEEK OUT YOUR PHONE LIBRARIANS

Along with your regular floor staff of librarians who interact with patrons every day, also make it a point to speak with the staff who answer questions over the phone.

Many library systems participate in a multilibrary consortium of phone support, so the people who supply phone help at your library may not in fact be located on your premises. If this is the case, see if you can speak to a supervisor at the phone bank or get direct access to the phone logs to see the kinds of issues that patrons are reporting.

Recently, I had the opportunity to get feedback on a new version of our online catalog from a group of librarians who are the operators on our phone support system. They had a very intimate knowledge of the problems faced by our patrons on the catalog, because they hear from the patrons who are struggling all of the time. Additionally, with screen-sharing technology in its infancy, their interface to help patrons with our most advanced systems is primarily an oral one, as they have to ask a battery of questions first to determine where on the website someone is and second to explain verbally the steps needed to rectify the situation. If key elements of the interface are buried an extra three or four clicks deep in the site, this is a frustrating barrier. The phone operators will know exactly where these pain points are and will often have suggestions for their improvement.

▶ CONSULT WITH YOUR INFORMATION TECHNOLOGY/SYSTEMS PERSONNEL

If you have in-house technology support, you will of course want to work hand-in-hand with them to get the most out of any technology project you install. Your information technology team is going to be most concerned with mitigating potential risks of a project, its cost, who's going to do the work to develop it, and who's going to be responsible for maintaining it on an ongoing basis.

It is imperative to have someone from your information technology team involved at the planning stage of a project. They will be able to guide you to avoid redundancies (e.g., using a similar existing application instead of building one from scratch), and they will make sure that any new technologies developed are deployed in such a way that they will be able to maintain them on an ongoing basis.

Maintenance is a huge issue; some industry conventions estimate that up to 80 percent of the lifetime cost of a piece of software will be maintenance (i.e., cost and effort after the initial development; Sun Microsystems, 1999). You may be able to build a neat new crowdsourcing web application in your spare time, but upgrading the server software, fixing bugs, backing up databases, scaling as it becomes more popular, and moving it to a new platform in a few years when the original language it was written in becomes obsolete—all of these tasks will likely fall to your technology support team. Having their full partnership at the outset of the venture will make that process easier and more manageable over time.

If you use outside resources for these tasks, make sure the documentation you give them is as clear and succinct as possible. Communicate to them any branding or style requirements, software version/platform restrictions, details for accessing your servers for staging, testing, and hosting of any completed work, and their contacts for getting paid.

► CONSULT WITH YOUR LEGAL EXPERTS

It sounds all well and good to talk about interacting with patrons and exposing the staff in new and different ways, but new ventures can raise some thorny legal questions. Libraries have traditionally taken a "privacy at all costs" legal stance that amounts to "don't ever share patrons' information." While there is some validity to this approach, it is at odds with the explosion of online sharing that many patrons have come to expect. It may turn out that one of the biggest obstacles to implementing some of these projects is that they conflict with or even flatly contradict your existing privacy policies.

Services like public staff profiles (employees' expectations of workplace privacy), social sharing among patrons (patrons' expectations of privacy within the library), and interactive subject guides (ownership of patron-generated content) have significant legal implications. See Chapter 7, "Best Practices," for more about the library policy implications of new types of patron engagement.

► GET MANAGEMENT SUPPORT

The senior managers of your library have the ultimate responsibility for the success or failure of your projects. Like the information technology folks, they are concerned with costs and risks, but they are also concerned with public perceptions. Management will be looking at the big-picture aspects of your projects, including:

- ► How does this fit in with the library's strategic goals?
- ► Is this project innovative? How does it compare to what our peer institutions are doing?
- ► Will the press be interested in covering it?
- ► Will donors be interested in giving money to further this project? Can we get grants for it?

Senior management will often ultimately make the call about when to get involved with emerging technologies, when to collaborate with other institutions, and when to not get involved (Rodger et al., 2005). The risk of implementing a type of project that hasn't been tried in your library before can be balanced with opportunities to reach new audiences or to find a way to keep up with change. Open and honest communication of both sides of that argument can be key to getting their backing for your projects.

Metrics are immensely helpful for making the case to senior management. Managers who think in big-picture terms (and may not be technically savvy enough to evaluate the innovation of a project on its own merits) will inevitably ask the question, "How do we know if this is worth doing?" By being able to point to hard figures, your projects will gain credibility. For web projects, visit and page view statistics are great, but engagement statistics (how many people contributed material in a crowdsourcing project, for example) are even better. See Chapter 8, "Metrics," for more ways to measure and report upon patron engagement.

▶ PROVIDE APPROPRIATE STAFF TRAINING

As technologists concerned with the experience you are delivering to your patrons, you will have the goal of creating new web features that can be easily understood when your patrons first encounter them. But no matter how intuitive your designs, it will be inevitable that some explaining will be necessary. Additionally, the users who are most familiar with your existing systems will likely be your staff, who interact with users every day out of necessity. It will be critical, then, to include enough time for the staff to be thoroughly trained so that they can offer the appropriate level of assistance to the public. If you have staff dedicated to training, get them briefed on upcoming projects as early as possible and coordinate schedules with them. Often, getting staff trained to use a new web system can be a bottleneck in the deployment schedule.

It is vital to test training materials with a sampling of actual end users of a given product. If they require more explanation, this may be indicative of places where more time should be allotted for training. Bear in mind also that instructions can be signals of design failure. If you have a form or other interactive web feature that requires a lengthy explanation, this is often an indication that the feature isn't well-designed in the first place and should be modified or redesigned.

▶ CHOOSE THE RIGHT SOFTWARE VENDOR

Good library software vendors are partners, but they are neither employees nor friends; they are in business to make money first and make the right choice for your library second. They will be critical to the success of your project, but it is vital to understand their motivations, which will differ significantly from those of the library.

If you are contracted to a software vendor to develop or implement a project for you, having clear goals specified on paper in a signed contract is imperative. No matter what is said in a sales meeting, vendors are under no obligation to deliver any more than exactly what you have contracted them for. If you ask about a particular feature you'd like to see and you're told "we're working on that right now," don't assume that means that feature will ever exist.

It's not that vendors are inherently untrustworthy but rather that their motivation is to deliver the product they were contracted to deliver as quickly as possible with the fewest complications. A clear up-front understanding, in writing, of what features will and will not be delivered by a certain date is the key to a happy, productive vendor relationship. Better to have some angst and negotiation right at the beginning of a project (where it's expected) than at the delivery deadline (where it's a problem).

5

IMPLEMENTATION

▶ **Create a Unified Library Web Presence**

▶ **Incorporate Social Media into Your Website**

▶ **Create and Offer Interactive and Collaborative Subject Guides**

▶ **Promote Your Librarians with Public Profiles**

▶ **Highlight Deep Collections and Reveal Them in New Ways**

▶ **Use Crowdsourcing to Create a Collection with the Help of Your Patrons**

As you might have gathered by this point, there is no one single project you can undertake or button you can press that will turn your library into a shiny new next-generation model. It can be argued (as we did earlier) that becoming a next-generation library is as much about a sensibility or an approach to the networked, information-rich world in which we find ourselves as it is about building some new websites. The following example projects should be approached as an inspiration and a tool for looking at your library through the lens of new technology.

The projects in this book are not a mandatory list, and if you fail to complete one of them, it will not disqualify you from the ranks of the "next-genned." There's not a lot of computer code or configuration instructions contained in these pages (you can view the companion website at http://www.alatech source.org/techset/ for more specifics); instead, it's a guide to the thinking behind what makes these projects relevant for forward-thinking libraries.

Additionally, the forces of technological and commercial change that are shaping the environment in which libraries exist are fluid and ever-changing. There are far more projects than can be contained here, some whose technical challenges are beyond the scope of this book. Mobile technology, for example, is having a massive impact on next-generation librarianship, but this topic is covered in detail in Jason A. Clark's *Building Mobile Library Applications* (THE TECH SET #12) and in a bonus project, "Expose Your Catalog's Best Features via Mobile Devices," on this book's companion website (http://www.alatech source.org/techset/).

▶ CREATE A UNIFIED LIBRARY WEB PRESENCE

To keep every cog and wheel is the first precaution of intelligent tinkering.

—Aldo Leopold

The first project in our list is an evaluation and cleanup of all of the websites and digital properties that will be seen by your patrons.

Prepare Your Site with a Next-Generation Audit and Cleanup

Libraries are awash in digital information in many forms. A typical library might have an online catalog, an informational website, sites for downloading audiobooks and e-books, a number of subscription databases, as well as perhaps an image gallery or two, a handful of promotional "brochure-ware" minisites, wikis, a staff intranet, and presences on any number of social media platforms. These sites are likely to have been created by different staff members (or outside vendors) over a period of years. Within an organization, librarians may think of each of these as a distinct and separate experience with its own strengths and weaknesses.

However, your patrons are less likely to make such distinctions and will not only perceive all of your separate digital experiences as simply "the library website" but will in fact be confused when their visit requires them to behave differently to navigate different sections of the site. Your goal, then, is to make your patrons always feel that they are part of your institution no matter which of your platforms they are currently visiting. In this project, we will take inventory of the entirety of your online presence, examine how all of its components relate to one another, and produce a new, unified presence across all of them.

Create a Project Inventory List

An absolute prerequisite to creating an integrated experience is knowing exactly how many of the different platforms your patrons see during a visit. The very first thing to do is to make a list of all of the public and internal websites owned by your library. A simple spreadsheet is an ideal tool for the task, preferably one that can be shared among all of the members of your team (such as an online Google Doc). The web inventory document should have columns to identify key information about each web property, including but not necessarily limited to the following:

- ► The **domain name** of the website.
- ► The **location of the server** for the site. Is it being hosted within your organization or externally? If externally, what hosting company?
- ► The **contact information for the site's administrator**. If you need to make changes, you'll need to know who has the password.
- ► The **contact information for the person responsible for the site's content**. This is not always the same as the administrator. In the case of a commercial product like a subscription database, this person will not even work at your library.
- ► The **contact information for the application developer**. This is the person you'll contact if you need to actually change the application code that runs the site.
- ► Whether or not the traffic on the site is being **tracked with any sort of metrics software**, as it will be important to know exactly how each site is being used currently.

Questions worth asking about each of your sites may include the following:

- ► **How many pages** are in the website? Not all sites are created equal, so the "footprint" of each will influence its place in the priority. Bear in mind that on a database-driven site, the number of pages served to the public may be radically larger than the number of actual files that make up the site; in this case, look at the number of records in the database.
- ► Is the site being **backed up** regularly? If so, where do those backups live?
- ► Who is **responsible for the content** on the site? (Note that this is usually a different person than the administrator.)
- ► How is the site **funded**? Are there any grant funding considerations to keep in mind? There may be special requirements to display certain information or to give credit to funders in a particular way.

If your institution is a small one (such as a local public library), then it may turn out that the list is somewhat easy to assemble, and the staff members responsible for the content are few in number (maybe it's just you!). It may also be the case that your information technology department may already keep such a list, so check with them first. See the companion website (http://www.alatechsource.org/techset/) for a sample Inventory Checklist document.

Make Your Third-Party Sites Look and Behave Like They Are Part of a Unified Whole

The online experience that you offer to your patrons extends beyond your website and online catalog. If you provide any third-party sites such as e-book vendors or subscription databases, you should treat them as if they are a full-fledged part of your website because that's likely the way your patrons are going to perceive them. Just because you happen to know that you pay a company every month to provide certain services from their web servers, that doesn't mean that your patrons will necessarily even know when they are leaving "your site" and going to "their site." Your goal is to make all the sites feel as unified as possible.

For each of the third-party sites to which you are linking, answer the following questions:

- ▶ Do the site's owners allow you to **edit the look and feel** of the pages?
- ▶ Do they allow you to **edit the global navigation**?
- ▶ Is the site **on brand**? (See the later discussion of auditing your branding, p. 42.)
- ▶ Have you watched patrons traverse **the connection between your website and the third-party site**? Were they successful? Did they know they were leaving your site? Could they find their way back?
- ▶ **Can you make changes** directly on the third-party site, or do you need to go through an intermediary? If so, have you documented the contact information for that intermediary?

One Easy Way to Manage a Website: Get Rid of It

You'll note that earlier I put traffic metrics on the mandatory part of the inventory list. This is because any serious evaluation of the worth of a website should be tied to the amount of use it gets. Traffic metrics are of course not the *only* measure of worth; some sites have importance to a narrower audience, and a lack of page views is not necessarily indicative of a lack of value.

However, it is a frustrating reality of web development that sometimes a lot of effort goes into the creation of a web tool that winds up hardly ever getting used. If you've been part of the team that built a particular website, it may be an uncomfortable, even emotionally painful truth to realize the great image gallery or archival discovery tool you and your team sweated months over is not seeing any use. It may be tempting to say, "Well, it's already built, so we might as well leave it up and running." But these are often the project sites that wind up over the years orphaned, with a logo three years out of date, broken links, and stale content. Left far enough adrift, they can actually harm the experience of the few users who do find them. It's often better to offer nothing than to deliver a bad experience.

Additionally, the breakneck pace of innovation in the world of the web means that, somewhere along the way, you may have invented a wheel that someone else came along and reinvented for you. Built your own video delivery system years ago? Say hi to YouTube. Custom-crafted a content management system in PHP? Drupal and WordPress probably did a better job of it than you. You may find that you're better off converting the content living your bespoke solutions to an open platform with a community of developers around it rather than continuing to swim upstream alone.

If you do decide to retire an old site that's no longer performing well, make sure that you archive its contents properly. Digital binary files (images, audio, and video) should be stored safely, and the contents of any databases should be dumped to a plain-text backup in a common file format (SQL or CSV). The proper procedures for the archiving of an expired website go beyond the scope of this book; see the companion website (http://www.ala techsource.org/techset/) for links to resources on the topic.

Going forward, any time you start a new web project, it is useful to give some thought to and document the retirement policy for a website, or even build in a "life span" to the project—a point at which it will be deleted if it is no longer in regular use. This might seem harsh, but the well-documented literature about the software development life cycle shows that over the full lifetime of a piece of enterprise, server-based software, a majority of the manpower needed to keep it running is spent not on the initial programming but on the maintenance to keep it running (Sun Microsystems, 1999). To look at it another way, updating server software, maintaining security patches, and backing up databases are all tasks that require the precious skilled resources of your technical staff that may be better used to create the new products that allow your library to keep moving forward.

Give Your Markup a Checkup

If you are technically inclined and familiar with the inner workings of HTML code, it may be worthwhile to examine the source code of your pages and determine how up-to-date it is. Even if you have no control over the code that runs your website, you can always see its output via the "View source" menu option. (*Note:* If you're an experienced code jockey with a deep respect for CSS and the <div> tag and a dog-eared copy of the Zeldman and Marcotte [2010] book *Designing with Web Standards*, feel free to skip this section.)

Like eating right and exercising regularly, maintaining clean markup has a host of healthy benefits. It is easier for your programmers to edit and for new staff to learn. It is also easier for search engines to parse; a good "scrubbing" of your HTML templates can actually improve your performance in popular search engines (more on this in a moment). And perhaps most importantly in the rapidly changing world of library technology, *good markup prepares you for the next thing that has not yet been invented.* Bringing life to your site's layout with JavaScript-based animation or displaying it on a shiny new iPad (or whatever Apple maddeningly replaces it with next year) is made much easier with a foundation of clean, standards-compliant code.

Start with a quick validation of a few pages from each of your sites. Validating the output of your webpages against the official W3C standards is a step skipped by many developers. It's easy to think of the markup as "close enough" because it looks okay in Firefox and Internet Explorer. But the status quo in the web world changes regularly, and many new innovations depend on the stable foundation of a valid code base. Code validators are plentiful, including free plug-ins to Firefox and other popular browsers, web editing software such as Dreamweaver, and online at the W3C's own website (http://validator.w3.org/). (*Pro tip:* If validation returns dozens of errors, start by fixing the first one on the list and work down; a lone tag out of place or unclosed will often throw all that follows off by one.)

Validation, however useful, will not catch issues that are technically correct but considered bad form. Much as water-stained ceilings or cracked brickwork are signs that a trained home inspector can use to point out that maybe you shouldn't buy that fixer-upper after all, there are telltale clues in the HTML markup of your webpages that can highlight potential problems. Here are a few:

- Recent web standards have required a **DOCTYPE** at the top of the page, which lets browsers know which exact version of HTML each page is using. "HTML 4 Transitional" or "HTML 4 Strict" are good. Any variety of XHTML is better. Earlier versions of HTML (pre-4) are bad signs. A missing DOCTYPE is an instant failure.

- Look out for any deprecated text-styling code in your HTML such as the **<font> tag** or items with align="..." attributes. These have no place in modern HTML as their function has been replaced by the purpose-designed and more powerful Cascading Style Sheets (CSS) language. HTML should describe each page's *meaning and structure*, while CSS should describe its *appearance and presentation*. Appearance-related code leaking into the HTML is to be avoided.

- Also, watch out for the overuse of **table tags for layout**. The <table>, <tr>, and <td> tags are perfectly good elements, as long as they are being used to present tabular data. If you see them being used simply to create the left and right columns on your pages, that's less correct. Tables that contain other tables are also a clue that the layout is less than optimal.

- Another sign of shoddy or outdated coding is **unquoted attributes**. From XHTML forward, the values of attributes in all HTML tags must

In October 2009, web developer and blogger Derek Powazek wrote a harsh critique of companies offering "search engine optimization" services. In it he states that the best practices for success in a search engine are increasingly indistinguishable from simply making good web sites. He closes the article thus:

> Which brings us, finally, to the One True Way to get a lot of traffic on the web. It's pretty simple, and I'm going to give it to you here, for free: Make something great. Tell people about it. Do it again. That's it. Make something you believe in. Make it beautiful, confident, and real. Sweat every detail. If it's not getting traffic, maybe it wasn't good enough. Try again. (Powazek, 2009)

In fact, the best way to optimize your pages for search engines is simply to follow a few rules of thumb, which will also improve your site's performance overall:

- **Encourage linking** to and from your pages. Perhaps the single best thing you can do to improve your pages' search engine ranking is to get other sites to link to your pages.
- Make sure that all of your **page titles** are clear, concise, and descriptive. The contents of each page's <title> tag is weighted very heavily by search engines. Additionally, it's what most search engines display as a link in their search results, and it's what your users see in their list of bookmarks after they add your page.
- Make sure you're using the **semantic markup** of HTML to describe the parts of each document by their function. Use <p> tags when actually describing a paragraph, not when you need a little bit of space. If you just need to mark up different sections of a page, use the semantically neutral <div> and <span> tags.
- Of special importance within semantic HTML is the proper use of the **header tags** (<h1>, <h2>, etc.). The purpose of these tags is to label each section of your site with a headline, and search engines take particular note of their content when they appear to be used correctly. There should be a single <h1> tag at or very near to the top of each page, and as many <h2>, <h3>, and so forth, tags as are needed to demarcate the sections of your site in outline fashion.
- Investigate the new section and navigation markup tags available in **HTML5**. If you're on the cutting edge and wish to experiment with the new HTML5 standard, it includes a few new semantic tags for denoting the parts of a page, including <nav>, <header>, <article>, <section>, <aside>, and <footer>.
- **Use care when naming URLs** in your site. Keywords within URLs make it easier for users to understand the purpose of a page and also count

for an increased search ranking "score" when a search term matches part of your address. Therefore, give careful thought to what you name the files and folders you create. If you use content management software such as Drupal that allows you to customize URLs, take advantage of it. A link like "http://library.org/locations/downtown" works better for both patrons *and* Google than does "http://library.org/loc.php?id=15."

▶ If you move a website and the addresses for old pages change, don't forget to create **redirects** to the new URLs so any previous bookmarks or search engine indexes can pick up on the change.

Finally, avoid the "urban myths" of search engine optimization. The "meta keywords" tag has not had significant impact on search engine rankings in over a decade. Likewise, the practice of cramming a page full of synonymous or loosely related words is ineffective. There are no gimmicks or shortcuts anymore; just make great, clean pages full of interesting content to which people want to link and then spread the word, and you'll be fine.

The web is, in fact, moving increasingly beyond the idea of pages and instead allowing for the exposure of the data that those pages represent. As an example, the website Schema.org, a collective effort of the major search engine companies Google, Yahoo!, and Microsoft, contains new guidelines for exposing the information on your sites as extractable, linked data without feeds separate from your HTML. For more on new trends in structured data and the Semantic Web, see *Semantic Web Technologies and Social Searching for Librarians* by Robin M. Fay and Michael P. Sauers (THE TECH SET #20).

Create Site Maps to "Deep Link" into Your Collections

There is, however, one way that the setup of your site has a very important impact on the ability of search engines to index your site. For a search engine to offer your pages in its results, it must first create its own index of the contents of your site, which it does by making a copy of your homepage, following every link on that page, loading each of those pages in turn, following all of the links on each of those pages, and completing the process (sometimes called "spidering" a site) until the text content of all linked pages is copied. This index is the raw material that becomes a page of search results.

However, this is a process that excludes a vast amount of the data you might have posted on the web. The main barrier to this search engine indexing is the POST request, which is a method of sending information from a user's web browser back to the site's server. It's what happens whenever you place an order on Amazon, send a message in Gmail, or post a comment on a blog.

It also happens to be the way searches are usually sent from the search box on your homepage to your library catalog. Because POST requests are never sent from search engine indexers, the only way that an individual item in your catalog will ever find its way into Google is if a regular web link exists from an indexable page to that item's page in the catalog. If the only way to a bibliographic record page in your catalog is via the search box, search engines will pass them by. *All* of them.

The solution? Create plain old web links in a site map directly to those bibliographic record pages, and leave them where search engines can find them.

In a collection with millions of items and frequent updates, it is not very practical to have pages lying around with millions of corresponding links. But it is well within reach to create site map pages full of links to certain key pages. Within a library collection, certain items are very popular while others are not used at all, and a chart based on popularity tends to follow a "power law distribution" whereby the most popular items in your collection make up a disproportionate share of all use. This means that improving links to a relatively small percentage of those most popular items will improve access to a very large portion of all requests for materials. Using circulation statistics or web analytics, make lists of your top 100 most popular items every month, or the top results from the 100 most popular search terms, and create pages that link directly to their catalog records. These lists can be made manually or scripted to run automatically using a bit of programming.

A simple way to create these site map pages is to post them on your library's blog. Patrons love lists, and a monthly "Most Popular" post will maintain your site's freshness for them while giving search engine spiders passage into the deep parts of your collection. (For further reading on the "deep web," see http://en.wikipedia.org/wiki/Deep_web.)

Examine Your Patrons' Account Experience

Most libraries require some form of sign-in to track which patron is currently using the system. While the log-in and account administration functions of your site might not seem particularly exciting, they actually form the heart of the most intimate online experience you offer to your patrons. Each wants to know about *her* current status: what books she currently has borrowed, when materials she has requested will be delivered, and what items are coming overdue. Additionally, the increasingly ubiquitous social networking sites such as Facebook, Twitter, and their brethren have set expectations among your patrons of what a personalized experience should be. If the log-in and account pages on your website are perceived as unhelpful or uninformative, you are missing an opportunity to reach your patrons at their most engaged.

To evaluate the experience of logging into your websites, there's no substitute for observing your patrons or just going through the process yourself. If possible, create test accounts for use by the staff, and distribute them to a number of different staff members.

If your library offers online sign-up (e.g., to get a library card at a public library), then create the accounts using the same interface that will be used by the public. Pay particular attention to the quality and informativeness of the messaging at every step of the way. Is it clear to patrons where to go to sign up? Is the sign-up form easy to understand? Once they have completed the form, is it made clear what patrons can expect to happen next? As the saying goes, you only get one chance to make a first impression. Exceed the users' expectations at the moment they choose to start participating, and you'll be off to a great start. Throw barriers in their way, and you may disappoint them right away.

If your library does not offer online sign-up (as in many academic libraries), then be sure that the messaging is clear for users who might need to acquire the proper credentials. If, for example, a student must have a valid student ID to sign in, direct them to the office that assigns the IDs. If your university library has a temporary guest policy, ensure that it is linked here as well. Make no assumptions about how prepared a visitor might be to participate.

Using the list of sites you created earlier, have patrons or members of your staff sign in to each of the sites in turn. Watch for signs of confusion, hesitation, or frustration. Are there links to a "My Account" homepage given on each? Are those links in a consistent location on each page? Does moving from site to site require a new entry of username and password each time? Are the usernames and passwords the same? If not, is it explained why not?

This last part, the single sign-on, adds a large measure of convenience for your users; once they have logged into the catalog, they can move to your blog, image gallery, or subscription databases and still be tracked as the same user without entering another password. It is fairly common in university settings (where it is used to keep one logged into the library website, student account pages, and academic resources websites) but less so in public libraries. The exact technical details of the implementation of a single sign-on mechanism are beyond the scope of this book. For now, just be aware that from the point of view of the library patron experience, every time your patron has to type in a username, library card number, or password, a small amount of inconvenience is adding up. If you observe your patrons having difficulty with managing their accounts and log-ins across different parts of your sites, it's an excellent thing to look for and report to your technical team.

Once the patron is signed in, consider the design of the My Account page. This page will quite possibly be the most frequently accessed page on any of your websites after the homepage, and it will certainly be the most relevant to the patron. Ask yourself these questions:

▶ **Is the account page consistent across sites?** If multiple sites (e.g., your circulating catalog and your e-book provider) have separate log-ins, they may also have separate account pages to manage them separately.

▶ **Does the account page offer useful help?** Using the account page to seamlessly answer the most frequently asked questions will remove some of the burden on the staff who currently answers those questions.

▶ **Are you using this page to promote other library services and collections?** While I certainly do not recommend burdening your account page with ads or unnecessary links, it is a frequently accessed page with very high engagement.

Enhance Your Website Branding: How Your Library Dresses for Work

One of the things that libraries can learn from the world of commerce is the importance of branding in creating a consistent experience for our patrons. An integrated visual and interaction "language" across all of your web properties goes a long way toward creating an experience for your patrons that feels effortless and professional. While the term "branding" might be associated with advertising and selling, it also has a lot to do with perception and emotional attachment with your institution. Think of it as the way your library dresses itself for work. These are some of the benefits of a unified visual presence:

▶ **Professional presentation:** Adherence to a minimum standard of polish communicates quality and style to your online patrons, which in turn influences their perceptions of the institution as a whole.

▶ **Improved usability:** By keeping navigational links and other cues similarly placed and styled from page to page, you lower the cognitive load on your users to orient themselves within a larger structure.

▶ **Emotional attachment:** If your institution has a strong brand presence, then any good experience your patrons have elsewhere in the institution will be in some small way intertwined with their interaction with the website. The identity of universities, for example, can be multifaceted, complex, and strongly branded; if the basketball team won a big game last week, or the university sponsored a concert on campus, the school colors and logo in the corner of each page will trigger a memory of a bit of that experience.

▶ **Consistent messaging:** Consistency in design is reassuring, and hearing the site speak with a single voice reinforces a sense of authority and reliability.

▶ **Navigation:** Library websites are hubs of online information, with thousands of links in and out. Letting people know when they are on your site and when they have left your site is important.

Audit the Current State of Your Brand

From the earlier clean-up exercise, you should have a good sense of the different websites that your library operates. Go through each site individually to make sure that they are being presented to users in a visually and navigationally consistent manner:

▶ **Are the colors, fonts, and logo consistent in their presentation?** Any brand identity for your institution should be specific.
▶ **Is the spacing of the layout grid consistent?** The underlying shape of headers, footers, and columns should be the same shape and size as much as possible.
▶ **Is there consistent navigation between the different sites?** Links between different sites and back to your main library website should not change in size, style, or placement from site to site.

Create a Style Guide

Check to see if your institution has a graphic style guide. If you're part of a university, museum, or other large institution, see if there is a graphic communications department. If not, see if you can track down the designers who designed your most recent logo, signage, and letterhead. Ask if this department has already created a style guide. (Speaking as a creator of these guides, I can tell you that if they have one, they will be ecstatic that someone is putting it to good use!)

A typical graphic style guide for the visual identity of your organization should indicate:

▶ how your **logo** should be treated,
▶ what **colors** should be used (often extremely precise),
▶ which **typefaces and fonts** are acceptable, and
▶ the **dimensions and alignment** of all branded materials (frequently, specifications for use of a logo include not just its appearance but also the amount of free space around it and its relationship to other items on the page).

Additionally, if the style guide contains information about the treatment of web/online visuals, it may include:

▶ **RGB** equivalents for all color choices (as colors on screen are specified differently from those in print),

- ▶ **substitute fonts** for use in web style sheets when the primary font is not available,
- ▶ the **placement of global navigation** items, and
- ▶ **wayfinding**—the ways of letting users know where they are in the structure of your websites, such as color coding by sections, hierarchies of headlines and type sizes, or "breadcrumb" navigation indicating depth within the structure of a large website.

A well-written style guide will be amazingly specific; follow its recommendations as precisely as possible for maximum impact. See the companion website (http://www.alatechsource.org/techset/) for an example of a completed style guide for visual identity.

Yikes! I Found Some Issues—Now What?

So, you've gone through the steps described and found that the markup is insufficient, invalid, or just plain bad. What happens next?

If you're responsible for maintaining your code, your next step is likely to dig in and start cleaning up. Most of the websites you'll be looking at are likely to have a main global template (or separate global headers and footers) that will be shared across most or all of your webpages. These are excellent places to start, because any changes you make to these templates will be carried across the entire site. You can work your way down from the most global to the most specific. Be sure to test frequently, however, as any changes to the global templates may have unintended consequences.

There are a number of excellent books and web resources that can educate you and walk you through the steps of modernizing the code base of your website. See "Recommended Reading" at the end of this book for some suggestions.

If you are not the person who does the coding, then use the documentation you've created to serve as a guide for your team's programmer. Take care to be thoughtful and objective about your critique, as he or she may have been the source of some of the code that contains the issues you're bringing up! There are often real-world constraints leading to certain design decisions during software development, and your coder should be given the benefit of the doubt.

What If I Don't Control the Website?

Unfortunately, because of the variety of websites used by each library and the vendors that provide them, it is frequently the case that you may not have full control over the code that comprises each site. In this case, it is important to communicate as clearly as possible what you would like to accomplish.

Even in the worst-case scenario, where your web software is tightly controlled within a closed, proprietary system and your vendor refuses to customize it, the thorough documentation that you have created in the steps described earlier can communicate the needed changes to them.

Software vendors who specialize in building library software do not hear from their end users often enough. If your efforts uncover problems, those problems stand zero chance of being fixed if that vendor does not hear about them.

Document Your Standards and Practices

If the steps outlined seemed second nature and the suggested audits turned up no issues, then congratulations! Your organization has well-run standards and practices in place and you can move on to the next project.

But if it was a struggle to track down the proper site documentation, the style guide was nonexistent, and the HTML code seemed to be written by 43 different people, each with his or her own idiosyncrasies, then what you've learned in this exercise has immense value to your institution even before you make any changes.

Spread your newfound knowledge by creating and sharing digital versions of the documents you've created. Post them on your organization's internal wiki or intranet so that they are available to members of the staff (and if your organization doesn't have either a wiki or an intranet, create one).

► INCORPORATE SOCIAL MEDIA INTO YOUR WEBSITE

Content isn't king. If I sent you to a desert island and gave you the choice of taking your friends or your movies, you'd choose your friends—if you chose the movies, we'd call you a sociopath. Conversation is king. Content is just something to talk about.

—Cory Doctorow (2006)

One of the most remarkable developments to result from the invention of the World Wide Web is the astonishing degree to which online social networks have permeated our society, creating a generation of library patrons for whom sharing conversations and interests has become second nature. In a relatively brief amount of time (less than a decade, really), the influence of online social networks on society has become remarkably deep and pervasive. In a 2010 survey from the always excellent Pew Internet & American Life Project, some 85 percent agreed with the statement, "In 2020, when I look at the big picture and consider my personal friendships, marriage and other relationships, I see that the internet has mostly been a positive force on my social world. And this will only grow more true in the future" (Anderson and Rainie, 2010).

One of the most fundamental impacts that social networking is having on libraries is that it is changing the way our patrons discover and share new information. It's possible these days not only to hear about a wonderful new book from a friend at a cocktail party but also to search your friends' preferences for recommendations online. Our patrons, while still wanting to control their own privacy, are also becoming increasingly comfortable with sharing their preferences online and will in fact feel thwarted when they want to share but cannot.

A quick personal anecdote: In my own browsing of websites, I don't think of myself as a particularly heavy sharer of content. Yet recently I was watching a short film about the fantastic personal library of inventor and Priceline.com founder Jay Walker, and when I realized that the film was hosted independently and not through a service like YouTube or Vimeo, I felt at a loss for how to share the link or save it. Even the extra step of switching to Facebook and cutting and pasting the URL into a sharing tool there felt like a little more hassle than it was worth. I could bookmark the webpage that contained the movie for myself, but I couldn't instantly *share* it. I suddenly realized how quickly I have become used to clicking the Add to Favorites icon on an embedded YouTube video or the heart-shaped "Like" button on ones from Vimeo. In my (admittedly mild) frustration, I learned a simple lesson: if librarians do not facilitate easy sharing of library materials via social networks, those materials *will not get shared* via social networks.

Consider the Three Types of Conversations

For libraries and other cultural institutions, the innovative thing about the new forms of social networking is that it allows free-flowing conversations to happen between the institution and its patrons in any direction. The following formulation of the types of conversations comes from Clay Shirky's excellent TED Talk presentation from June 2009, which can be viewed at http://www.ted.com/talks/clay_shirky_how_cellphones_twitter_facebook_can_make_hi story.html.

Most obviously, the conversation can flow **from the institution to the patron**. This is the traditional model, where the institution speaks and the patron listens. Social media can be used in this way, and it frequently is. However, this just reinforces the way in which institutional messaging has traditionally happened: from the top down. While posting advertising-like messages on your Facebook fan page or Twitter feed can be an effective way to broadcast announcements, it is not a particularly interesting way of having a conversation.

The conversation can also flow **from the patron to the institution**. Where previously there might have only been a suggestion box by the circulation desk or a contact form on the website, patrons are now empowered to respond publicly in a variety of ways.

Finally, the real revolution in social networking is the ability for patrons to have **conversations about the institution with each other**, independent of the institution itself. This is where the new kinds of social networks are making things very interesting indeed.

When making the decision how to engage your patrons in conversation via these tools, here's a sobering thought to keep in mind: these conversations are going to happen *whether you choose to participate or not.* That's the revolutionary bit about that third type of conversation—we have passed the point where communications need to be blessed by central authorities to happen at mass scale. The decentralized, ad hoc, amateur mass conversation is a new thing, but it's here to stay. This is the key point for the decision makers at your institution to grasp: you can engage your patrons in these forums or not, but if you do not choose to engage, you are not precluding anyone from participating. They'll happily go on *without you.*

Set Up Accounts on Social Media Sites

If you haven't already done so, your first step is to create accounts on the major social networking and social media websites. The most popular ones are almost always completely free, so signing up takes only a few minutes and an e-mail address. Even if you haven't quite decided how to use these networks, it can't hurt to have good account names reserved. This is especially the case if you'd like your account name to be a short, memorable acronym. On Twitter, for example, the convention is that directing a message to a particular person is done by spelling out their screen name. We were fortunate to scoop up @nypl early on and not get stuck with something like @newyorkpubliclibrary—that's 16 more characters out of Twitter's allotted 140 that our patrons can use to reply to us! Even if you're unsure if you'll be using Twitter, if you see that a good short variation of your library's name is available, snap it up today.

When creating accounts for these third-party sites, a good practice is to have your IT department create "placeholder" e-mail addresses that will forward to any appropriate staff members and use these rather than individual staff members' e-mail addresses. That way, if there is staff turnover or someone goes on extended leave, the social media account administrative messages will not disappear with them.

Consider Flagships versus Satellites

If your library is a small, private one with a single location, a single presence online will do the trick. But if you're part of a large urban library or a major university, then there are likely dozens of departments and hundreds of staff who'd like to have their voices heard. How, then, to find the balance?

Many large institutions (mine included) have embraced the idea of a central flagship account for the main institution, while allowing divisions or locations within the institution to also participate with their own voices. The main "brand" can communicate and converse about the big stuff, while smaller "boutique brands" can speak to their own audiences. The Smithsonian Institution, for example, maintains accounts for their primary si.edu brand, but each of its component museums also has its own social media accounts. The Library of Congress promotes itself on flagship accounts but links to numerous projects within its walls, each with its own identity and voice, on its social media page (http://www.loc.gov/homepage/connect.html). At the New York Public Library, we have Twitter, Facebook, Foursquare, and Tumblr accounts for the library as a whole, but a large number of our 90 branches and many of our research divisions, from the Map Division to the Bronx Library Center, tweet and blog to their own specific audiences.

Choose Platforms on Which to Participate

If you or your institution has not previously engaged in any social media platforms, the choices can appear a bit daunting. Here is a brief overview of the different types of online social networks and the most popular examples of each.

Sites whose main purpose is **social networking** exist primarily to allow people to communicate with others. These are what most people think of when they hear the term "the social network." As of this writing, the two most popular are **Facebook** (with more than 600 million active users worldwide) and **Twitter** (with over 200 million users).

Facebook is the "800-pound gorilla" of the social networking world, as well as the subject of everything from countless parodies to an Academy Award–winning film. Facebook uses a double-opt-in system for any two users to become "friends" (one person initiates the request and the other has to accept it), at which point the two friends can share personal information and links online. For an organization such as a library, Facebook provides public "fan pages" which can be populated with your content. Having a Facebook fan page for one's library should be almost a prerequisite of any social network interaction, because Facebook is where your audience is likely to be, especially in the younger audience of an academic setting (Ganster and Schumacher, 2009).

Twitter uses a different, asymmetric model of network creation, where any user can follow others simply by clicking a "follow" button, and reciprocation is not necessary. Twitter also traffics mainly in "tweets," short messages limited to 140 characters (including spaces and punctuation). Sometimes the butt of jokes and mocked for shallowness, Twitter has millions of devoted fans who testify to its utility. The brevity of messages requires posters to get to the point, and the asymmetric model of "followers" makes it an excellent way to follow people whose work you admire in order to keep up with what people in your profession are talking about and using. It's also an excellent way to share links to specific information. Libraries that would like to experiment with Twitter should just sign up for a regular free account. Be advised, though, if you're out there, people may start following you and conversing with you right away! Twitter has a particular feel to it, a vernacular that is difficult to explain but easily learned by practice. If you're planning on "tweeting" for your library, you might want to learn the local lingo and idiosyncrasies on a personal account first.

As of this writing, software giant Google has just released **Google+**, their latest entry into the social networking arena, and they seek to offer their users finer control over sharing privacy through the creation of "circles" of friends and acquaintances. By the time you read this, it should be readily apparent whether or not they have succeeded.

Aggregators and **link sharing networks** are largely built around the sharing and commenting of links. Aggregators are plentiful, but some of the most common include **Digg**, **Reddit**, and **StumbleUpon**. These networks depend less on networks of friends and colleagues, and more on rating or ranking sites by votes. For example, Digg allows its users to "digg" a link (basically the same as a Facebook "like"), but then the main Digg.com website keeps track of the score of each link and allows you to browse the top-ranked links in any number of categories. Libraries can most easily participate with these sites by embedding the buttons used to vote for a site on any page you think patrons would be interested in sharing.

Social media sharing networks encourage participants to create their own media and share it with others. **YouTube** and **Flickr** are perhaps the best known, as they are the largest sites for sharing video and still images, respectively. YouTube is by now familiar to almost anyone who's ever watched a video online, and its tools for embedding, sharing, and promoting are unrivaled. A strong suite of custom "channel" creation and statistics-measuring analytics make it ideal for a library on a budget.

Flickr in particular has a very user-friendly set of sharing tools and is perhaps the best example of a media-based site that also allows the spontaneous creation of self-organizing groups around that media. A recent offshoot of Flickr of great interest to libraries is the **Flickr Commons** (http://www.flickr .com/commons), a section of the website devoted to historical, largely public domain photography from the collections of more than 40 cultural institutions around the world. You can link to Library of Congress and New York Public Library case studies on the companion website (http://www.alatechsource .org/techset/).

Other social media sites with broad appeal include **Vimeo**, a video-sharing site with lovely usability and a strict noncommercial policy that results in a more creativity-friendly environment, and **Tumblr**, a variant on blogging sites that encourages the posting, sharing, and resharing of short, visually engaging images and text.

Another web application that is not generally thought of as a social network but in fact pioneered many of the innovations (such as tagging) that made Web 2.0 happen is **Delicious**. This "social bookmarking" site is simple but ideal for sharing recommended links. A library-curated list of links with short annotations can be published or embedded on your websites to easily generate trusted lists of recommended web destinations for your patrons on particular topics.

Some of the most recent and interesting social networks are **locational networks**, which encourage the sharing of information based on physical locations. The current most popular of these is New York–based **Foursquare**, which uses a mix of web and mobile app technology to allow people to "check in" at their favorite locations. If you aren't familiar with Foursquare, you might be surprised to find that your patrons have been checking in there for some time!

Some new locational networks such as **HistoryPin** or **Sepiatown** are combining time, history, and images to create searchable archives of historical pictures, integrated with browsable maps and geographic locations. While not social networks per se, they offer libraries immense opportunities to share historical visual content.

Keep an Eye on Trends

These are a few of the most popular sites, but there is no guarantee that today's most important social networks will remain so. Many have come and gone (Friendster, anyone?), and there's no reason to expect that we won't see new entrants onto the scene in the future. Don't hop on every new bandwagon that comes along (everyone wants to be the next Facebook, and some of the newcomers have poor implementations but a healthy PR budget to convince you that they're the next big thing), but you should listen for new developments. I don't consider myself an early adopter, but I do follow a "three times rule": if I hear about a new platform or piece of software from three unrelated people I trust (say, a friend, a work colleague, and someone I follow on Twitter whose opinions have tracked closely to mine in the past), then I will investigate it further.

It is critical to also use your web analytics software (see Chapter 8, "Metrics") to keep track of the platforms from which you are getting the most referring links. The percentage of traffic from each rises and falls over time. If you notice a drop in StumbleUpon traffic and a rise in Reddit, ask yourself if there's a reason that such a change might have occurred and investigate further. And if you see a sudden jump in referrals from a new platform you've never heard of before, pay attention—you might be seeing signs of the next big thing!

Additionally, social networks also vary by geographic region. The sites I've mentioned here are the top ones in the United States, but traffic to European or South American library sites may well come from a completely different set of sites. There's no substitute for looking at your own web traffic reports to see which sites are truly sending you the most visits.

Make Sharing of Your Collections as Easy as Possible

Patrons' reasons for "liking" or "tweeting" vary widely. Some want to recommend items to their friends. Some prefer to highlight the goofy, funny, shocking, or crazy. Some may be trying to impress people. Some use social media as a kind of bookmark for oneself, using Twitter and Facebook to capture content they don't want to forget. As social networks become the preferred way for millions of people worldwide to collect and share things in which they are in some way interested, many choose to stay logged in to these sites as they surf around the web. This enables any site (including yours) to leverage a user's Facebook (or other) account by adding Share, Like, or Bookmark buttons to their own web content (see Figures 5.2, 5.3, and 5.4).

While it is possible to "hand code" all kinds of these buttons onto your website, an easier and more practical approach is to install them via a toolbar provided by a third party. A number of software products can take these sharing buttons from different social networking platforms and aggregate them into a single tool. A very popular one is the sharing widget offered by **AddThis.com**, a snippet of JavaScript code that can be embedded on any page on your website. Creating an AddThis account and installing the widget provides direct links to the sharing features of all of the most popular social networking sites, each in its own vernacular: a "like this" button for Facebook, a "tweet this" for Twitter, a "bookmark this" for Delicious, and so on. The AddThis widget is configurable and typically shows two or three buttons for the most popular platforms with an expanding palette offering two-click access to dozens of less-popular offerings. When patrons interact with the AddThis bar, they are

▶ Figure 5.2: Social Media Sharing Tools on the *New York Times* Website

▶ Figure 5.3: Social Media Sharing Tools on a BiblioCommons Library Catalog

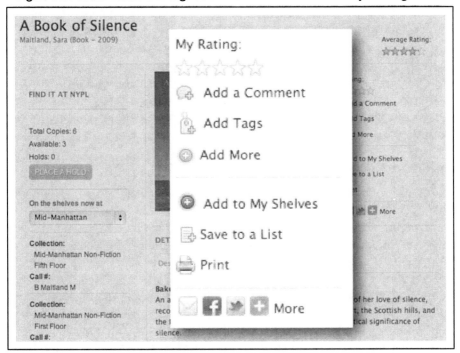

▶ Figure 5.4: Social Media Sharing Tools on the Library of Congress Website

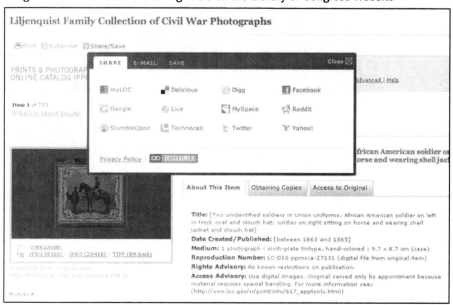

prompted to log in to their own personal account on their chosen platform (Facebook, Twitter, etc.), or, if they are already logged in, the item is instantly shared. There's no need for the patron to register with either AddThis or your library; the service simply leverages any social networks on which your patron is already participating. Additionally, by signing up with a service like AddThis, you get access to a set of incredibly useful and revealing administrative dashboard reports showing at a glance which items and pages on your site have been shared the most and which social networks are accounting for the most sharing.

Decide What Items to Encourage People to Share

You can never give people too many opportunities to share the items in your collections. There is a school of thought that posits that every single page on your site should be shareable. However, you will maximize engagement if you place sharing tools in sensible places nearest the items that are most likely to be shared.

To do this, look for your website's "nouns" rather than the "verbs," as people like to share the objects in your collections. You should therefore add social sharing tools to pages for bibliographic records (starting with every item in the catalog), archival materials, pictures in your picture collections, and any audio and video materials. Additionally, make sure that the basic information about your library is shareable: pages for any of your locations with maps and hours, event listings, and class sign-ups.

If you are blogging, make sure that sharing tools are added to every blog post, as well. Library blogs frequently contain some of the most timely and interesting information that you'll ever make available. Blog posts about interesting findings from your archives or engaging events at your library are the most likely pages to "go viral" and get passed around via social networks. In 2010, the two webpages that drove the most referral traffic from social networks and other sites to my library's website were a pair of blog posts, one of which highlighted a page from a 1941 teen magazine showing the wardrobe of an average college co-ed, and another in which one of our librarians listed every book that appeared in the television show *Mad Men* (with links to the catalog records, naturally). Without sharing tools in place, neither of these posts would have made quite the same impact.

If you're on Twitter, an excellent rule of thumb is to ask yourself before posting a tweet, "How retweetable is this?" A retweet, if you're not a Twitterer, is when one person re-posts on their own account a tweet originally posted by someone else. It's not stealing, nor is it exactly a form of quoting either; it might most accurately be described as an endorsement of sorts. Frequently, retweets are how things go viral on Twitter, as users can pass on an interesting tweet to all of their followers with the press of a button. A single compelling item, succinctly described and linked to, is a more likely candidate to be passed along in this fashion than a vague "Check out our new website!"

Pull Media from Social Networks onto Your Site

One way to broaden the impact of the social media sites with which you are participating is to pull content that has already been posted on those networks back to your main website and incorporate them there. For example, if you have started a Twitter feed to tweet the current status of what's going on at your library, those short, timely messages add up to a significant stream of what's going on right now and recently that would also be of as much use to your web visitors who are not Twitter users. Twitter offers an embeddable "widget" that can be installed onto any webpage (by adding the appropriate supplied HTML tags and JavaScript code). This widget will then display a box with the most recent tweets from a particular account. This has the double function of letting the Twitter-savvy know that you're participating and displaying a constantly updated stream of short updates to those who don't care a bit about what Twitter is.

Similarly, the photo-sharing site Flickr offers a suite of embeddable photo galleries that will let you display particular groups of images on any page of your websites. Share images to a gallery on Flickr, and, as a bonus, your main website will automatically update along with that gallery.

Follow Social Network Best Practices

Social networks may be third-party websites, but, despite that fact, many offer a degree of customization of look and feel. You should ensure that any branding graphic elements are correct according to your style guide (as discussed earlier): logos should be consistent and up-to-date; colors should match your official colors; and any text descriptions should be current and informative. The degree of customization offered by these sites varies widely. Facebook allows you to post your own images and text, but colors and background imagery are unchangeable from Facebook blue and white. Twitter, on the other hand, lets you change the colors and background of your page. Many sites allow you to upload a profile picture, which is often used in links to your page. This picture will often be scaled down to icon size, so make sure that it is sufficiently bold and simple to be legible at a much smaller size (see Figure 5.5).

Another important lesson is to use each social network for what it's best suited. Facebook fan pages are excellent for event announcements. Twitter is a great medium for responding to individual followers and promoting other pages. Flickr is the place to post images from recent in-library events. Don't feel like you have to post the same information everywhere. Rather, you should get a feel for the advantages and disadvantages of each platform and make your posts on each complementary.

As social media platforms have increased in popularity and importance, the task of managing an organization's message across platforms also becomes more important. However, the staff time demands of managing that conversation require increased effort as more and more of the conversation about your library takes place outside of your walls. It's important to use effective tools to follow and engage in what's being said on social networks.

A good first step is using search engines to search what's being said about you, but take care to use meaningful searches. The general Google search is far too broad to return meaningful results, as search for your library's name will likely turn up a lot of your own websites! A far more effective approach is to use Google's News search, which will list anything posted recently on news sites

▶ Figure 5.5: Examples of Twitter Profile Images That Read Well at Small Sizes

from mainstream news organizations to popular blogs. If an event or webpage from your site has gone viral, it'll likely show up in the news results. Google News Alerts can be configured to e-mail or text you when stories for particular keywords are posted; if your library gets written about only intermittently, having the Alert tell you when stories appear is a better use of your time than obsessively checking Google News manually in vain every day. Twitter's own search is also a useful tool to see what people are saying about you right now and which of your links they're sharing. Twitter allows you to save particular searches and also to subscribe to them as RSS feeds, which is particularly useful if you use a newsreader application to read large numbers of blogs.

Other venues to keep an eye on are the aforementioned news aggregators such as Reddit, Digg, and MetaFilter. Each of these sites works a little differently, but, in general, they are communities built around rating, sharing, and filtering news according to the collective opinions of their users. If you're getting traffic from these sites, you've likely garnered some significant attention elsewhere on the web already. They're great places to stay up-to-date with more general industry topics (e.g., you can search them for "library" or "digital humanities" to see articles and websites that the users of these aggregators have voted most popular, useful, and relevant).

A recent type of tool has emerged that is custom-tailored to the task of tracking and managing messages across multiple social media platforms. One of the most popular of these so-called dashboards is **HootSuite** (http://hootsuite.com/), which started as a tool for managing content on Twitter but has evolved into a way to publish a particular story on everything from Facebook to Twitter to Flickr to blogs while tracking and measuring responses. Social media dashboards can be real time savers, and the companies that make them are inventing some very innovative ways to view, respond to, and measure the conversation to and between your patrons as it moves from inside the library out onto the web.

SocialFlow (http://www.socialflow.com/) is another overview tool that our library has found useful. It is used to monitor your social presence in real time (on Twitter, Facebook, Google Buzz, etc.) and even goes so far as to suggest the ideal times to launch particular messages to maximize their impact.

Think It Through: Have Your Policies in Place

Once you have decided to join the conversation, make sure that your library has a policy for dealing with the newfound conversations that will happen. It's not a frightening prospect, but the new omnidirectional conversations afforded by web-savvy, well-connected patrons should be considered before jumping in with both feet.

The first policy to consider is identifying the staff within your organization who can participate in social media. The policy regarding participation in social media at my library has evolved over time. From the beginnings of social media through early 2008, there was no formal policy, but informally it was assumed that senior management approval was necessary to start blogging or using social media on the library's behalf. However, a later revision of the policy flipped that standard, and we encouraged our staff to participate in social media. This led to a period of interest and innovation among our staff. Despite a few minor episodes where staff posted less-than-professional content on a professional public channel, the most engaged staff were generating wonderfully creative content on our blogs and Twitter feeds. That led to the current policy, where we've developed an internal class in blogging and social media that staff are strongly encouraged to attend before posting on behalf of the library, after which they have relative autonomy.

The specifics of the policy are that librarians or any staff member with a public service component to his or her job is encouraged to post, with the approval of a supervisor, as long as the topics on which they are posting advance the library's purposes and further the library's mission. Librarians are expected to post within their area of expertise. Librarians are also required to identify themselves as a library employee. For more on developing your library's social media policies, see *Strategic Planning for Social Media in Libraries* by Sarah K. Steiner (THE TECH SET #15).

Be Mindful of Privacy and When Sharing

Libraries, on the whole, are immensely concerned with the privacy of the personal information of their patrons. And this is as it should be; there are enough countervailing business forces at play pushing more and more private information, willingly or unwillingly, into the public sphere. Public libraries are one of the few institutions that can act as a counterbalance to the self-interest of corporations and other organizations that would love to dig into the private lives of individuals.

Facebook's somewhat mixed record on personal privacy issues puts it at odds with many libraries on that front, and I would not encourage any use of Facebook (or any third-party social network, for that matter) that requires library patrons to sign up for a particular social network to use library materials. However, for the vast number of patrons who do already use these networks on their own time, offering tools to promote sharing via these networks can be a mutually beneficial one; for patrons who wish to share library materials with their friends, the tools make it easier, and the library gets additional promotional exposure through the trusted network of a personal recommendation.

A good rule to follow is to use third-party platforms as vehicles for sharing but not to require them for core participation. Adding a Facebook Like button as a convenience for Facebook-using patrons squares with the policies of most libraries, but building, as an example, a new search tool that would require a Facebook account as a prerequisite for its use would not be a good idea. In my own work, I would draw the line at requiring any of my patrons to sign up for a third-party account with any service with which my library did not have a formal agreement.

Promote Your Social Media

Now that you've done the work of creating web-based tools and venues to participate in a conversation with your users, the last step is to make sure that they know you're there. After all, a conversation is useless if no one participates!

Your first step is to create a single page on your website with a central set of links to all of your presences on social networks. If your website has a set of secondary navigation links, such as in the footer of each page, linking from there to this social media page is a good idea. If your institution is larger and you have multiple presences on each platform (the "flagship and satellite" model mentioned earlier), you can either dedicate this page to the flagship accounts or get more creative in presentation. The Florida State University website, for example, has a very clean page offering links to their Facebook, Twitter, YouTube, and LinkedIn presences for every department in the university (http://www.fsu.edu/socialmedia/; see Figure 5.6).

If your library generates a lot of print materials, make sure that links to your social media efforts are included. Just as in the previous decade it became commonplace to add URLs to print advertisements, it is now common to see Twitter "@" addresses (or even hashtags) or Facebook page links to print materials. If you have flyers printed up for events, make sure to include social media links along with web addresses and other contact information.

In-library signage can also be used for this purpose. At NYPL, we printed out small 4-by-6-inch cards promoting the links to each of our social media properties and posted them in elevators, on bulletin boards, and at other prominent locations.

E-mail signatures are another great, easy place to add links. If you sign your e-mails with your address or phone number, add a link to your Facebook fan page and to your Twitter feed to encourage anyone you e-mail to click through.

But the most important way to encourage use of social media is the direct approach: make it easy! The steps we have taken earlier in this chapter to install easy-to-use sharing widgets on key pages will likely go the furthest to encourage participation. The nature of social networks is such that people

▷ **Figure 5.6: The Social Sharing Overview on Florida State University's Site**

enjoy and participate in sharing from friends, colleagues, and other like-minded individuals. This will lead to organic growth as your linked material spreads from person to person, one at a time. If you're interested in delving deeper into the details of incorporating social media into your library practice, see *Strategic Planning for Social Media in Libraries* by Sarah K. Steiner (THE TECH SET #15).

▷ CREATE AND OFFER INTERACTIVE AND COLLABORATIVE SUBJECT GUIDES

Wikipedia only works in practice. In theory it's a total disaster.
　　　　　　　　　　　　—Anonymous *Wikipedia* volunteer (Gardner, 2010)

The Internet has long held the promise of a universal communications medium, where every receiver of information can also be a creator. Early on in the lifetime of the web, only the power users and alpha geeks were the ones who knew how to post their own content. But the past decade has seen the fulfillment of that early promise, and now it is almost trivial for anyone to post text, pictures, audio, and video to the web. It's a fundamental shift in the way the public we serve expects to interact with information. One way libraries can profit and learn from that shift is to move beyond simply posting content approved or created by their staff and instead interact with and encourage participation from patrons. Subject guides can be interactive in the sense of being frequently updated and interlinked with other web content or in the sense of being able to be written, edited, and adapted by individuals in their intended audience.

Wikipedia is the seventh largest site on the World Wide Web, and, as of 2011, there were more than 82,000 active contributors working on more than 17,000,000 articles in more than 270 languages (Wikimedia Foundation, 2011). Despite the fact that it's completely built by volunteers and freely editable by anyone who views it, it has been found in numerous surveys to be at least as accurate (if not more so) than traditional encyclopedias and other general reference sources (Giles, 2005). In fact, a 2006 study found that expert researchers actually rated the accuracy of *Wikipedia* higher than did nonexperts (Anderson, 2007).

The great lesson of *Wikipedia* is that deep knowledge of a particular subject may reside in the minds of many who are not experts, have no desire to be paid for their services, but merely wish to share their knowledge. Many of the same engaged, informed contributors to *Wikipedia* are also among the patrons of our libraries, along with many others like them who will be encouraged to contribute in the future. This is a resource of vast capability and one that we have only begun to tap.

By creating your own subject guides using tools that allow your librarians to rapidly adapt to a changing information landscape, link to resources in image, audio, and video formats, and collaborate in concert with patrons, you can take advantage of the passions and knowledge of your audience and convert them from passive receivers into active participants (Dalbello, 2004).

Decide on a Subject for Your Guide

You should identify topics, collections, or subject areas in your library that are particularly well-suited to posting in an interactive subject guide by virtue of availability or interest from librarians or members of the public. Just as the best cooking starts with the best, freshest ingredients, the best subject guides start with excellent subjects. When initially creating a subject guide, ask the following questions:

> ▶ **In what subjects are your patrons most interested?** Ask the frontline librarians and reference staff which collections are most requested.

Check your website's logs of searched terms, both externally (what people are googling to find your site) and internally (what people are searching for on your internal search tool once they have arrived at your site).

▶ **For what collections is your library renowned?** Most libraries have areas of focus or subjects they cover better than others.

▶ **Do you have materials of local interest?** Local history is always a popular topic.

▶ **Do you have collections that are underused?** What do you wish more patrons knew that you had? Responding to demand is good, but a subject guide can also drive interest in particular collections, especially once it is linked to and indexed in search engines.

Choose Your Weapon

Depending on what type of interactivity you'd like to have in your subject guides (staff-edited vs. collaboratively edited), your needs, your desired outcomes, the size of your audience, your level of comfort with software installation, and your budget, there are a number of possible ways to build an interactive subject guide. A few common solutions include the following:

▶ The popular commercial library-specific product **LibGuides** offers tools for adding lots of linked content in many formats and managing your guides among your staff, as well as being able to respond quickly to feedback from your patrons.

▶ **Wikis** are an easy way to get content online and are the best model if you want to allow collaborative editing with your users. Wikis are maturing as a platform, and will be familiar to many people.

▶ Subject guides can be quickly created in many of the popular open source **content management systems** (CMSs) popular with libraries, such as WordPress, Drupal, and Joomla. These platforms come with a certain amount of infrastructure out of the box, such as user accounts, editing screens, and the ability to create relationships between different types of content.

▶ Finally, there is always the option to build your own **subject guides** either using a hosted, template-driven solution like Google Sites, or creating in plain HTML. While this solution might be the cheapest and quickest to set up in the short term, it will be harder to maintain, change, and grow to scale.

See Chapter 2, "Types of Solutions Available," for in-depth information on each of these possibilities.

Seed Your Guide with Content

Once you have chosen a software platform and approach, get your guide off the ground by filling it initially with the best possible content you have available. Most libraries have a large amount of subject guides that have been written in the past and are in print or in a non-web digital format yet are still very well-written and relevant. These materials make a great starting point.

If you're planning on using a wiki approach for your subject guide, this does not mean that your patrons are going to write the guide for you. You will find the level of engagement and community interest increases if you lead with the strongest, most compelling content you can provide. After all, the best guides will attract the smartest and most expert readers, who will in turn make the best contributors.

Remember Your Mantra: Link, Link, LINK!

I am a firm believer that the hyperlink is one of the most underrated inventions of the twentieth century. This little snippet of markup code—<a href="some-address">Text to make into a link</a>—has revolutionized the way we interact with, well, *everything*.

If I had to choose a single rule to guide the development of an interactive subject guide, it is this: "Link to the stuff you're talking about!" While auditing a number of old sites at my library, I recently came across a folder of early online subject guides that had been posted to our website. They were digital transcriptions of earlier book-length descriptions of the highlights of our collections, organized by broad subject areas. These guides make for fantastic reading and offer incredible insights into the hidden treasures of the library. Digitizing them and putting them online must have seemed like a can't-miss prospect. So why were there no less than three versions (a late-1990s framed version, a later PHP-based version, and most recently a wiki version built on the MediaWiki platform) languishing unused on our intranet servers? Well, quite simply, no one had ever gotten around to adding links to the contents. On the web, it is expected that a page purporting to be a research guide should in fact link to the item it describes. These guides described items in our collections (many of them rare or unique) and then offered no additional help in finding them. The same resource but now containing outbound links to the catalog record of each item and the descriptive page of the collection or division that houses it would be used constantly.

If your library is like ours, sitting on great descriptions of your collections that aren't on your websites, they're a great place to start. If you have any existing research guides, finding aids, or other descriptive materials that are in digital text form but not necessarily web-ready, an excellent project to encourage participation from your users is to post those raw texts on the web and get people to help you format them and add links. If a collection guide describes key books, add a link to the catalog records for those books. If the guide describes how to use a particular database, link to the database. If a finding aid describes a recently digitized collection, link to the scanned document and its metadata.

Avoid Common Pitfalls

There are a few guidelines to follow in order to tilt your online subject guide toward "beloved" status and away from "abandoned." First and foremost, **avoid "digital cul-de-sacs."** Don't tease your readers by describing an item or resource in the collection but not letting them click through to it. Follow the advice earlier and make sure that any key descriptions of materials link more deeply into the collections. A particular offender in this regard is the PDF document. PDFs are wonderful for a lot of things, especially for packaging a well-formatted document for eventual printing on paper. But they are lousy at being webpages. A plain old HTML webpage has a number of advantages over a PDF document: it's searchable, easy to cut and paste from, and can easily be embedded with links clickable from a browser. I hear you saying, "But I put links in PDFs all the time!" Nope, sorry—they are not as easily navigated as web links, and different browsers deal with PDFs differently, so a document that might open in a window on one browser might get saved to disk on another. Furthermore, the fixed page size of PDFs make on-screen scrolling and navigating difficult. If the purpose of your guide is to direct people more deeply into collections or description of collections that are on the web, you want links from a browser window. Saving a document as a PDF and posting it online is not a substitute.

Second, **don't forget to cultivate a community.** Just because you've created an interactive tool doesn't mean that you'll automatically get participation. Setting up the software is the easy part; encouraging people to participate takes effort. See Chapter 7, "Best Practices," for a deeper look at cultivating community around your projects.

Don't write too much. Guides should, well, guide. A good guide contains just enough information to get you to the materials in a library collection. If the guide itself becomes large and complex, the purpose of the guide is undermined.

Don't link to too many things. Here again, the purpose of your subject guide is not to present an exhaustive list of every resource on the topic. In the field of usability, there is a rule of thumb based in research on human cognition that states that seven items (plus or minus a couple) is the magic number; with less than seven items, we can perceive each item on the list as an individual, but over seven items, we just start to see "lots of things" and get overwhelmed. If you have a list of more than seven items, either break it up into two lists or remove a few.

With collaboratively created subject guides, it might be the case that one of your participants may break one of these rules. Rather than reject or rebuke their contribution, this is actually a good opportunity to engage. For guidance of how to do this, examine how the contributing members of the *Wikipedia* community flag problematic entries and encourage cleanup of suspect postings. Often, even if a contribution is flagged as "Citation needed" or "Please help improve this article by adding reliable references," the offending entry will not be edited or removed but left as an appeal for the addition of authoritative sources.

Have Your Policies in Place

If you choose to create a wiki-style subject guide or otherwise take in content created by patrons, make sure that your library's policies are clear about moderation and ownership of content. See Chapter 7, "Best Practices," for more details on creating a policy for patron-generated content. For more on interactive subject guides in general, see this terrific online guide: http://www.libsuccess.org/index.php?title=Subject_Guides.

▶ PROMOTE YOUR LIBRARIANS WITH PUBLIC PROFILES

The most important asset of any library goes home at night—the library staff.

—Father Timothy Healy

By now, you will have gathered that one of the themes of next-generation librarianship is that librarians are participants in a conversation rather than just gatekeepers of stored knowledge. A way in which libraries can lead by example is to create an online profile for each librarian. Regular visitors to physical library locations may develop relationships with the librarians at the service desks just by seeing their faces, but, without a name, biography, or other context, that relationship can remain fleeting and dependent on who was working the desk that morning. Profiles can allow patrons to learn more about the depth and breadth of expertise of the whole staff and be more selective about the librarians with whom they interact.

Profile pages have a multitude of benefits for a library. In the context of webpages, they perform an important emotional role, establishing a more personal connection through the digital medium and reinforcing that the content found on the library's website is being written, edited, and compiled by humans and not simply machine generated (see "The Power of the Personal Appeal" below).

Librarian profiles can also reveal librarians' areas of expertise. A casual researcher might be more likely to engage a librarian in conversation on a research topic knowing that the librarian is knowledgeable in a related area.

The profile pages make an excellent "node" in the library network to aggregate all content created by an individual. These pages can serve as a platform for the dissemination of articles, blog postings, or research guides written by a librarian, deepening the communication of expertise.

Crucially, public librarian profiles are useful not just to the public. Staff can use them to learn about their colleagues and therefore know who to contact for particular types of questions. The more staff know about each others' professional skills, the better they can serve their patrons by more effectively referring queries to the most appropriate staff member.

The Power of the Personal Appeal

People respond to messages better that appear to come from other people rather than institutions. *Wikipedia* has done in-depth surveys of the performance of their fundraising banner advertisements and found that far and away the most potent appeals are the ones from *Wikipedia* founder Jimmy Wales and particularly the banners that feature his face (Wikimedia Foundation, 2010). Wales' smiling face, ubiquitous during the fundraising drives, outperforms even ads featuring other famous people. *Wikipedia* doesn't speculate why the Wales banners are so popular, saying only that the data is unambiguous. But one can hypothesize that personal appeals from those directly involved in a project carry extra weight in making a connection with the viewer. Public librarian profiles can help create that kind of personal connection.

Decide What Content to Include in a Profile

The whole point of a public profile is to get the identity of the librarians out there, so including a name is essential and pretty much goes without saying. Beyond the name, though, there's any amount of information that can be added to the profile (see Figure 5.7).

The librarian's **job description and responsibilities** help to communicate to the patron what kind of work the librarian does. Bear in mind, however, that most patrons will probably not know the exact distinctions among the different job titles used within a library, so be sure to also indicate what types of questions are best handled by a given staff member.

A librarian's **education and credentials**—degrees earned, certificates, and the like—would certainly be appropriate information to convey on a profile page, especially if those credentials are in relevant fields of study. However, it

▷ Figure 5.7: A Typical Librarian Profile Page (Brown University)

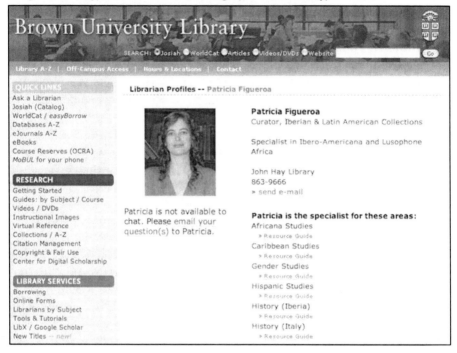

is probably far more useful to the patron to learn about the librarian's **areas of expertise**. What kinds of questions is the librarian particularly good at answering? Who's better at helping with genealogical queries? Help with science research? Finding a job? Over time, librarians tend to find their niches and become the "go-to" person within the library for particular answers. A short summary of these areas is immensely useful to the patron.

Don't forget to include any **languages spoken** other than English on the profile. Non-native speakers may find the library less imposing if they know that they can find someone to converse with in their native tongue, and the public profiles will allow them to seek out this information on the web in advance of their visit. This information can also be useful to other staff members to find a translator on the fly when dealing with a walk-in patron who speaks little or no English.

Of course, there should be all relevant **contact information** on the profile page. The decision of whether to include individual phone numbers and e-mail addresses is at the discretion of the library, but if these pieces of information are not posted on the profile, at least indicate the location where the librarian works (both building address and desk or floor location within the building) with general contact information for that building. Profiles should also remind users if a librarian is available for one-on-one consultations, as this service is generally underpromoted by libraries that offer it.

If your library encourages its librarians to post on blogs, create **links to each librarian's posts on the library blog**. If your software supports it, or your web programmers can make it happen, a listing of "All posts by this librarian" can form an incidental archive of interests and subject expertise that automatically updates over time, serving as an organically growing extension of the profile itself.

Similarly, if policies allow it and the librarian wishes to share them, you can include links to each librarian's **personal blogs or social network accounts**. While it's not likely that a librarian would like to encourage patrons to friend them on Facebook, there are a multitude of librarians who post about industry-related topics on sites like Twitter and Tumblr or their own personal blogs. This should be an exclusively optional step, of course, but afforded if the librarians want to promote themselves this way.

Even if a librarian does not want to link to other personal sites, allowing space for a short **biography** will give space on the profile for hobbies and other nonacademic interests. Librarians, on the whole, are an interesting bunch of people who frequently have lots of interesting things going on outside of work. Do you knit? Ride mountain bikes? Play bass in a punk rock band? Write novels? Competitively solve crossword puzzles? Well, guess what—so do many of your patrons. This is a perfect opportunity to create emotional affinities between librarians and patrons and to break down the institutional facade a bit.

Finally, **photographs** also make a huge difference in the effectiveness of public profiles (Newell, 2004). Humans are hard-wired to respond to faces, and a simple photograph alongside a short profile goes a long way toward maximizing engagement. According to Darcy Duke at MIT Libraries, usability testing has shown that users were much more likely to contact librarians if they had a photo attached to their profiles and subject guides. Some staff may be sensitive about posting pictures of themselves. Duke says that at MIT, some of the staff there were initially "a bit reticent to use photos—not because they didn't want their photo on the web, but they just didn't like any pictures they had (originally we asked them to provide their own photos)" (Darcy Duke, e-mail interview with the author, January 17, 2011). Since then, MIT has provided their librarians the option of having professional headshots taken, which has made the staff more willing to post a photo. If your library does not have access to professional photography, the abundance of good-quality digital cameras means that it is easy to take your own headshots. A plain, monochrome wall in a well-lit hallway away from direct sunlight makes a good studio. Shoot with a low-light setting without using the built-in flash (to avoid harsh light), and get up close enough that the head nearly fills the frame. And don't forget to smile!

Choose a Software Platform to Use

Many existing software platforms that you may already be using at your library will support librarian profiles. If you look around, it is likely that there's already an easily configured piece of web software you can use to create and maintain your profiles:

- ▶ The **LibGuides** software includes easy tools for posting public librarian profiles and associating them with particular content.
- ▶ **Blogging or content management software** like WordPress, Drupal, or Joomla often have a "user" content type that can be made public and turned into a profile page. Both LibGuides and CMS software are the preferred solutions, because they will facilitate the automatic relationship of content to the profiles of its creators.
- ▶ Many varieties of **wikis** allow logged-in users to create public profile pages, but, even if this isn't available, it is easy to create a wiki page for each staff member, especially if you have a smaller staff. Consult the usage documentation for your particular wiki software to see which approach will work best.
- ▶ If you're part of a university, check with your technology support team, as there may be a **campuswide profile system** into which you can tap.
- ▶ Finally, it is always an option to **build your own profiles** as static HTML webpages. You won't get the benefit of the automatic linking between content and profile, but, if you have a small staff and limited resources, this might be the most low-cost, low-effort way of quickly getting the profile information on the web.

Refer to Chapter 2, "Types of Solutions Available," for an in-depth look at the advantages and disadvantages of these different types of software.

Create the Profiles and Keep Them Current

One of the important considerations in creating staff profiles for the first time is determining who will create and update the content in the profile pages. The preferred method is for each librarian to have the ability to write, edit, and post their own profile. This approach requires that the software platform you've chosen supports individual user accounts so that the staffer can log in and make their own changes. If you decide to take this approach, make sure that the process is well-documented, and offer a sample profile page to give your staff an idea of what a completed profile looks like and to ensure consistency.

However, if your frontline library staff is under significant time pressure from their other responsibilities, it might be more effective to appoint a single person to gather all of the profile information and do all of the data entry at once. Individuals can then edit their own profile as needed.

Promote and Use the Profile

The creation of a profile page for each librarian is only the first half of the project. Once the profiles have been established, they should be woven into the content of your library's website and online catalog.

An easy first step is to create a **staff directory** page that links to all of the available profiles at once (see Figure 5.8). How much information you present for each person on this page depends on how large your staff is; if you have, say, less than ten people on your staff, you might be able to post everyone's full profile on this page and minimize clicking around. If you have several hundred people on staff, you'll probably want to cut it down to just names (although in that case use headers and subheaders to create meaningful groupings, as a long alphabetical list of names is a fairly useless way to navigate through your staff). If possible, this page should include names and pictures, as well as a minimum of information (such as areas of expertise and languages spoken) to offer the browsing visitor some context clues.

You should also be sure to link to the profiles from your intranet or other internal website, and **encourage staff to read one another's public profiles** so that they can get familiar with each other. Don't assume that patrons are the only ones who need to know about your staff; public profiles are also a way to get them to know about each other. When staff are encouraged to fill in their own profiles, they frequently share information that is of interest to their coworkers. As an example, the internal profiles we posted on my department's wiki taught me that one of my coworkers writes novels, another rock-climbs, and a third wrote a book about the history of my mother's hometown. But, more importantly, staff profiles do more than just let each other know about shared hobbies—*they improve public service.* The more you know about the skills, education, and areas of expertise of your colleagues, the more you know about where to refer patrons for help and from whom to learn new skills.

And just as the links from a staffer's profile to content created by that staffer reinforce the perceived expertise of that individual, **links from blog posts and research guides** to their creator's profile lend credibility and cross-reference to the content. This interweaving of content and profile helps to create a community of practice around particular topics and lead patrons to

▶ **Figure 5.8: MIT's Directory of Librarian Profiles**

practitioners with specific expertise. Once public profiles are available, using them to unify all content created by that librarian deepens the web of shared interest and scholarship inherent in the library's staff.

Be Mindful of Privacy Issues When Encouraging Staff Participation

Concerns are sometimes raised around public librarian profiles in terms of privacy and exposure, especially from staff who might be reticent to participate. And it is true that before starting on this project, it's a good idea to make sure that your particular implementation of profiles squares with any library policies and procedures, and appeal to management to adjust those policies if you find that they are in conflict.

However, the libraries and librarians we have spoken with who have implemented profiles on their own have found very little cause for real-world concern, given that staff already have a visible public position within the physical library and the information contained on these profile pages has little if any sensitive information. As always, communication is key. Ask your staff for their input during the implementation, and be sensitive to concerns. Don't require anyone to include information that they are not comfortable publishing on the web. For your part, make sure that you are presenting the positive benefits: more engaged patrons, better service, and so on.

► HIGHLIGHT DEEP COLLECTIONS AND REVEAL THEM IN NEW WAYS

Every prominent document, every tapestry and map, or cigar box or menu, is there in the library because it was, at some point, someone's great happiness, some breathing person's joy, a thing about which he or she would say, "You have to come look at this."

—Will Eno (Llewellyn, 2011)

At the core of the current networked revolution is the astonishing property of digital materials to be instantly and perfectly copied. Once a text, image, sound, or moving picture has been converted to digital format, it can be transmitted, reshaped, and recontextualized almost limitlessly for very little effort or expense. This creates an area of immense opportunity for librarians to take digitized materials and promote them outside of the confinement of the library catalog.

There is an abundance of powerful yet simple off-the-shelf blogging and sharing tools that can be used to create feeds of content and promote them on the web. Librarians can use these tools to call attention to the breadth and depth of a library's collections.

How, it is often asked, can librarians encourage deeper research in the world of Google and *Wikipedia*? Part of the job of next-generation librarianship is to be an advocate for the deep collections that may not be exposed in public search engines. The common refrain is that "Google doesn't show you everything," and librarians tirelessly advocate for the digital resources, such as nondigitized archives and subscription databases, that their institutions make freely available within a library's walls but are just beyond the reach of search engines (for either technical or commercial reasons).

Yet while librarians can present examples of deep research, there is no reason that this presentation needs to be stuffy or academic. The stories behind artifacts in collections can be personal, compelling, rich, and meaningful without being steeped in jargon or catalog-speak. Putting a single artifact in front of a visitor and giving brief context can be an equally powerful experience for a professional historian as it is for a high school freshman.

An incredibly easy way to express the value hidden in your collections is by giving a rich, detailed view of a small number of items. While a traditional research guide endeavors to describe the whole of a collection with some detail, by picking a singular artifact and telling its compelling story, you can make the deep web instantly relatable, entertaining, and even fun (see Figure 5.9).

Keep It Simple

There is no need to get overly complicated. A single artifact with a compelling story makes a far greater impact than a fire hose of amazing things. While there is value and necessity in enabling searching and browsing of entire collections, sometimes the solitary item can speak much louder and in a more relatable fashion.

For inspiration, look at the way that museums display their collections. Most large museums have veritable warehouses of artifacts, with the majority largely out of public view. But within their galleries, they carefully curate the best, most striking items, placing them for maximum impact on the viewer.

It's also good to have a narrower focus or organizing framework to the presentation. "Cool things in the University Library Collection" is good, but "Letters from the University Library's Music Archives" might be better. Make it a "Manuscript of the Week" or "Photograph of the Day." Have a focus and a purpose.

▶ **Figure 5.9: An Infographic of Co-ed Clothing Choices from 1941, Reproduced in the Most Popular NYPL Blog Post of 2010 (http://www.nypl.org/blog/2010/01/24/ clothing-choices-1941-and-today)**

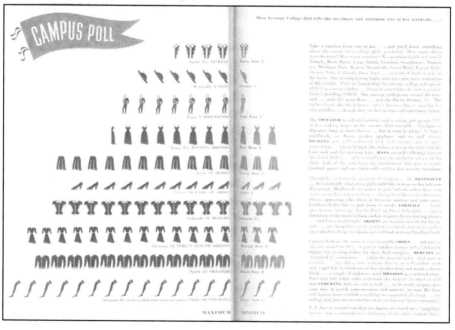

Choose the Items to Feature

To effectively promote individual items, choose from the things whose stories are most likely to resonate with your visitors. Ask the following questions when looking for items to feature:

What are the rarest or most unique items in your collection? If your library has any holdings that cannot be found in other institutions, those are excellent items to feature. Note that often the rarest items in a collection are not books; paper ephemera, prints, photographs, maps, and letters are more likely to be rare or unique and also lend themselves quite well to telling their stories in a short post. A recent study of the holdings of the 25 largest public libraries in the United States found that close to 90 percent of their materials are held by five or fewer institutions (Lavoie, 2011). There is a remarkable amount of unique content in our materials; don't assume that your library only has things that other libraries hold.

Do you have collections of local interest? If your library doesn't have much in the way of unique holdings or special collections, post things that are more personally related to your patrons and staff. Local history is always a popular topic, as is information about local ethnic populations. Local takes on food and genealogy are always a hit. Are there books relating to your town or region that contain stories of personal interest to your patrons? Can you make connections between things your patrons are personally proud of—a baseball team, working in the old mill, a regional dessert treat—and items in your collections?

What are your patrons' areas of interest? The things that are most frequently requested by your patrons will give you hints as to what might be popular and compelling if promoted. Ask the frontline librarians and reference staff for ideas about frequently requested collections. Another abundant source of patrons' interests is your logs of search terms, both externally (what people are googling to find your site) and internally (what people are searching for on your internal search tool once they have arrived at your site). See Chapter 8, "Metrics," for more information on tracking search terms.

Conversely, **what collections are underused?** Ask your staff this question: What hidden gems lie within your holding that you wish more patrons knew about? You can encourage use by featuring items from little-used but compelling collections.

What do you have already digitized and at hand? The purpose of this exercise is to expose collections, not create work. If you have recently had piles of musical scores or handwritten letters scanned, start posting some of the more interesting ones, and link them to their catalog records. Expose what you have.

Finally, **what is of most interest to you personally** as a librarian? The opinions of librarians matter to our patrons. If a librarian has a love of jazz, or crafts, or glassblowing, or medieval armor, encourage them to post their favorite items from the collection while briefly explaining why those items are personally meaningful. Illustrate the connection between an individual's passions and the treasures of your library's collections. An enthusiast's passionate take on a collection is worth ten dispassionate research guides.

Get Inspired by Three Sites That Do This Extremely Well

The Milton Glaser Archives at the School of Visual Arts in New York City contain the papers, notes, and works of the prolific illustrator and graphic designer who is perhaps best known as the creator of the iconic "I ♥ NY" logo but has produced decades' worth of other boundlessly creative works. The archivists responsible for this trove recently created the website Container List (http://containerlist.glaserarchives.org/), using standard Textpattern blogging software (see Figure 5.10). Each post features a selection from the archives with a minimal amount of commentary. With its simple design of black, sans-serif type on a white background, the site lets the vibrant, happy

▶ Figure 5.10: Container List

colors and bold lines of Glaser's work leap out at the viewer. Additionally, the tagging and dating tools built into Textpattern add a "semiformal" layer of metadata to the public collection. Beth Kleber and Zachary Sachs, the archivists at the Glaser Archives, chose Textpattern for its intuitive user interface and more stringent typographic and schematic standards compared to other blogging software such as WordPress, which, in Sachs' words, "speaks to our librarian-ness" (Beth Kleber and Zachary Sachs, e-mail interview with the author, March 19, 2011).

One can also look outside of the library and archives world to find examples of blogs and websites that focus on particular subjects and formats to maximum effect. One of the most venerable is **BibliOdyssey** (http://bibliodyssey.blogspot .com/), a blog run by Paul Kerrigan using the standard Blogspot software with little or no modification. BibliOdyssey features images of rare and wonderful old books provided by cultural institutions around the world, with multiple large images per post and a minimal amount of commentary written by Kerrigan himself (under the pseudonym "peacay"). Each post is organized on a single topic: an artist, a cultural collection, a type of book, or a subject, each chosen by Kerrigan's sophisticated curatorial eye and presented simply (see Figure 5.11). BibliOdyssey has proven so popular that it spawned a companion book in 2007, *BibliOdyssey: Amazing Archival Images from the Internet* (coauthored by Kerrigan and published by Fuel Publishing), thus becoming a book about a website about old books. The formula that makes it work, however, is simple to replicate: pick great items from a collection, and put them front and center.

Another spectacularly engaging site run by an individual is the wonderful **Letters of Note** (http://www.lettersofnote.com/), which describes itself as "an attempt to gather and sort fascinating letters, postcards, telegrams, faxes, and memos." Started on a whim by freelance writer Shaun Usher, the site has become extremely popular. Posting roughly once a week, Usher features a scanned letter (sometimes with a response from the recipient) followed by a plain-text transcription (see Figure 5.12). Writing only a simple introduction to set the scene, Usher lets the artifacts speak for themselves, and speak they do, telling stories ranging from hilarious (Conan O'Brien's response to a teenager's request for him to attend her prom) to thought-provoking (William Safire's unused draft speech for Richard Nixon to deliver in the event that the 1969 moon landing failed) to heartbreaking (a letter from Marilyn Monroe to her psychiatrist in the last year of her life).

What do these three examples have in common? First, they **let the artifacts speak for themselves**, often framing them with a bare minimum of descriptive text—one or two sentences, then the item itself.

▶ **Figure 5.11: BibliOdyssey**

BibliOdyssey

Books~~Illustrations~~Science~~History~~Visual Materia Obscura~~Eclectic Bookart

Tuesday, June 28, 2011

The Book of Knighthood

Miniatures cropped from the ~1460 manuscript containing Christine Pizan's *'Épître d'Othéa'* (Epistle to Hector; sometimes known as the Book of Knighthood) - Cologny, Fondation Martin Bodmer, Cod. Bodmer 49, courtesy of the Virtual Manuscript Library of Switzerland [link].

THE ANNOTATED ARCHIVES OF BIBLIODYSSEY

Add BibliOdyssey

to Russian
Translation

Search BibliOdyssey
Google™ Custom Search

Second, they **don't let their designs get in the way**. The page layouts are simple and clean, without clutter, so that any images come to the forefront.

Third, they have a focused, easily comprehended theme. They don't attempt to be all things to the whole collection; rather, they stay focused on a narrow swath of territory and become stronger for it.

Finally, they promote easy sharing of the posting. As seen earlier when we discussed incorporating social media into your website, each featured item is frequently "likeable" on Facebook or "tweetable" on Twitter with the press of a button, encouraging wider dissemination of the stories told outside of the boundaries of the library.

► Figure 5.12: Letters of Note

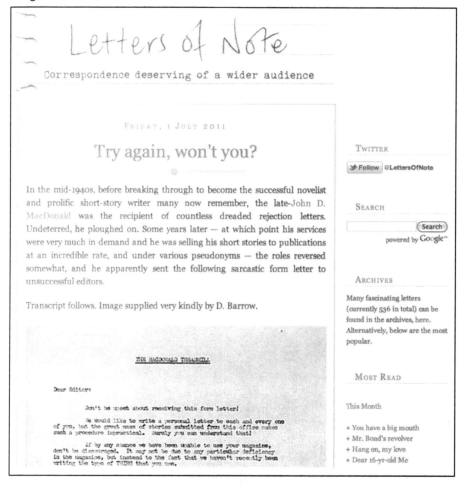

Set Up the Tools

Technically, this is one of the easier projects to complete in this book, as the simplest way to create a "visible archive" like the ones described earlier is to use standard blogging tools. There are a number of options that are free of charge, easy to set up, and surrounded by active communities of users from whom you can get help and learn new tricks. Here are some popular choices:

► **WordPress** is notable for its ease of use and variety of customization options, offering numerous optional plug-ins to handle different types of media. It is available as a hosted service or downloadable software you can install on your own server.

▶ **Blogger** is Google's free online blogging software. A bit less flexible than WordPress, it has the advantage of simplicity and ease of use.

▶ **Tumblr** is a very visually oriented type of blogging service built around the sharing of images.

▶ **Drupal** is a popular open source content management system. Drupal is more complex and proportionally more difficult to set up but ultimately more powerful and flexible than other types of blogging-only software.

There are many others; see the companion website (http://www.alatech source.org/techset/) for an updated list. There's also the possibility of writing your own custom software, but why bother? The blogging software listed here are rich enough in features and mature enough in stability that you'd be foolish to try to re-create them. If your library is already blogging and using a platform that supports individual "channels" for particular bloggers or groups of bloggers on a particular topic, then there's likely not even a need to install any software, as you can simply create a new channel for the effort.

Make sure that the software offers an RSS feed so that viewers who use newsreader software such as Google Reader have an opportunity to subscribe to your site and receive updates on an ongoing basis. Newsreaders have become increasingly popular as users find them a useful way to manage large amounts of information in a standardized format.

Leave Them Wanting More

Recall, if you will, the last scene of the movie *Raiders of the Lost Ark*, in which the Ark, now "safely" in the hands of government "experts" has been sealed into a crate, and we see it being wheeled into a vast warehouse filled with other crates of all shapes and sizes, receding into the distance and out of sight. It's meant to be a little joke to end the movie about gray bureaucracy triumphing over the nonstop adventure we've been treated to for two hours. But it also fires the imagination—if there's such an amazing object in *one box*, and this room contains *countless other boxes*, then how much other amazing stuff is in that warehouse? Watching that movie at age ten, I remember wondering if all the other boxes are filled with cleaning supplies, and the Ark is lost yet again? Or are there other equally astonishing things in each box? It was a wonderful way to end the film and, for me, a window into how the unknown works on our unconscious minds when our amazing pattern-matching brains get a glimpse of something special peeking out from just behind the curtain.

That built-in curiosity is hard-wired in our brains. Use it to your full advantage. Pick one favorite item from your library's collections, something odd, colorful, weird, artistic, historically significant, emotionally moving, or just meaningful to *you*. Put it on display where everyone can see it. Tell people why you, as a librarian, think that it is worthy of attention. Then remind people that you have a whole library full of similar things. Human curiosity will do the rest of the work for you.

▶ USE CROWDSOURCING TO CREATE A COLLECTION WITH THE HELP OF YOUR PATRONS

Joy's Law: No matter who you are, most of the smartest people work for someone else.

—Bill Joy (*Wikipedia*, 2011)

One of the most exciting innovations on the web in recent years are "crowd-sourcing" projects in which loosely coordinated groups of people from all around the world can contribute to a project in a single focused location. The ability of many people to quickly come together, each contributing a small amount of content, to create a coherent whole is something relatively newly afforded by the World Wide Web.

In a very broad sense, the web itself is a crowdsourced project, where anyone with Internet access and a text editor can create an HTML page just by following a few standards. And the idea of open participation from all comers to build a common good certainly applies to *Wikipedia*, the most successful user-generated, self-correcting information resource on the web today.

But crowdsourcing in the library, museum, and archives world is often taken to mean something a bit less grand in scope and more focused. I have found it helpful to sometimes refer to crowdsourcing projects as "microvolunteering," with the idea that patrons can contribute assistance to the library in as little as a few seconds if they like.

Learn from Great Examples of Crowdsourcing Projects

Despite a wealth of successful examples already in existence, crowdsourcing is still in its infancy. To understand the potential, it helps to take a look at a few of the most successful of the current, still early efforts.

The **Old Weather** project (http://www.oldweather.org/; see Figure 5.13) takes thousands of ships' logs from voyages in the early twentieth century and encourages the user to transcribe the ship name, date, latitude and longitude, weather, and other key information in order to build a historical record of patterns of trade and weather. This database will be of use to historians and researchers of all kinds. The project sounds, to be honest, terribly dull. However, Old Weather is notable for the way in which it incorporates narrative and game-play elements into the very act of transcription. It allows visitors who transcribe the logs of a particular ship to become part of its

▶ Figure 5.13: Old Weather

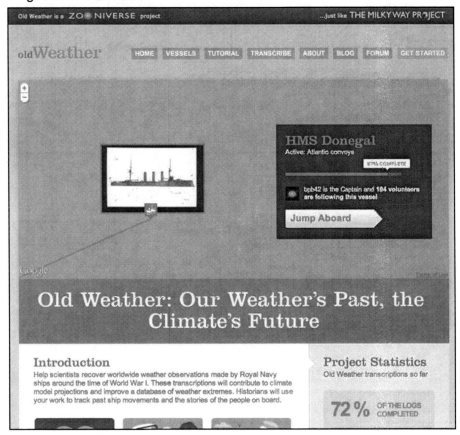

"crew," and the user who transcribes the most logs from one ship becomes that ship's "captain." Completed log entries are immediately located on an interactive map, revealing the ship's passage visually. Through clever design and well-chosen constraints on the kind of information that can be entered, it takes what could be a dull, menial task and turns it into an ever-revealing narrative.

The U.K. newspaper the *Guardian* recently launched a very successful "citizen journalism" crowdsourcing project that encouraged their readers to pore through the public expense receipts of members of Parliament (http://www.guardian.co.uk/politics/mps-expenses; see Figure 5.14). The more than 700,000 documents posed a formidable, mind-numbing obstacle for the reporters who would have had to have waded through them to discover any potentially newsworthy items. Their approach was to scan all of the documents and post them online for anyone to view, at which point the viewer could mark

▶ Figure 5.14: The *Guardian*'s "Investigate Your MP" Project

---

guardian.co.uk

News | Sport | Comment | Culture | Business | Money | Life & style | Travel | Environment

News ❯ Politics ❯ Investigate the MPs' expenses

Investigate the MPs' expenses 2

As the Guardian is reporting today, more than 40,000 further pages of MPs expenses claims have just been released. Help us go through the documents to find the best stories. We'll be adding more MPs and assignments as the day goes on.

In June of this year, Parliament published more than a million documents relating to MPs' claims for household and office expenses. The Guardian made it possible for nearly 25,000 people to get involved in reviewing the documents, in our groundbreaking collaborative project to investigate MPs' expenses.

Today a new batch of documents, relating to 2008/09 and the first quarter of 2009/10 are released. We've updated the mechanism to make it simpler to use, but again invite you to join us in digging through the claims. Just hit the button below to start reviewing, or find out what we've learned so far

Start here

Help us confirm the most interesting finds

2,393 pages, 2,393 have been reviewed.

Start reviewing »

Please read our privacy policy / terms of service

Recent discoveries - all discoveries

The Sky Sport debate

Other assignments - all assignments

---

the documents as "interesting," "nothing to see here," worth looking at," and so on. This first pass of all of the documents guided the newspaper's staff to potentially interesting findings, from which they ultimately produced a series of articles bringing to light fraud, mismanagement, and corruption (Andersen, 2009).

Many crowdsourcing projects are built around image collections, which often defy machine readability in a way that text might not. A great example can be found at the **Victoria & Albert Museum**'s website (http://collections .vam.ac.uk/crowdsourcing/; see Figure 5.15). A recent redesign of their online galleries found them settling on a consistent grid of square images for the photos of the over 140,000 items in their collections. However, the images (and, of course, the objects themselves) were a variety of shapes and sizes, most of which do not fit neatly into a square crop. Given the choice of letting a machine crop the images arbitrarily or having a poor intern crop

▶ Figure 5.15: The V&A's Crowdsourcing Page

images day and night for the next decade, they chose a third option: let a machine crop the images five to ten different ways, and simply ask the public to click on the one they think looks best. Dead simple, fast, and instantly intuitive. (In fact, the first time I checked out their site, I looked down at their "progress bar" and realized to my surprise that I had approved 36 images before my concentration wavered even a little!)

One of my team's contributions to the field is the New York Public Library's project to transcribe and categorize all of the menus in its extensive collection of historical restaurant menus. The **What's on the Menu?** (http://menus .nypl.org; see Figure 5.16) project encourages visitors to help transcribe the dishes on the menus into an organized database of dishes. While some of the dishes might have been transcribable via optical character recognition (OCR) methods, the menus varied widely in their layout, presentation, and legibility. Furthermore, we wanted to create a searchable database of dishes (as distinct from section headings and other descriptive text on the menus' pages) complete with prices and currencies, so simply pulling all of the text in by automated means would not quite be sufficient. After writing our own custom software for the task, we "soft-launched" a beta version of the website in April 2011; within a month, over 250,000 dishes had been transcribed off of over 5,000 menus.

These are just a handful of ways in which crowdsourcing techniques are being used. With the rise of the web, expect the number of examples to grow

▶ Figure 5.16: What's on the Menu

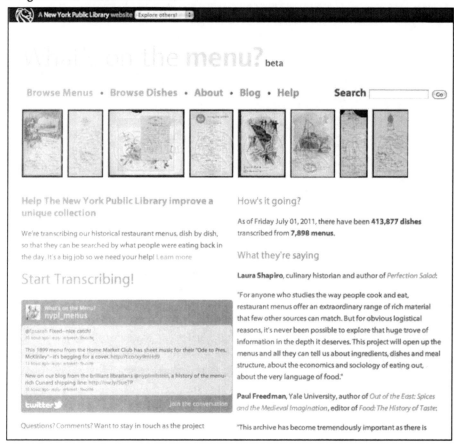

exponentially. The power of the web to capitalize on the contributions of its users is, as we speak, outstripping our ability to take advantage of that power, creating a vast, untapped resource as long as we have engaged, loyal patrons who want to help us.

Understand the Taxonomies of Crowdsourcing Projects

A recently published paper (Oomen and Arroyo, 2011) analyzes a number of crowdsourcing projects and proposes categorizing them into six types. Oomen and Arroyo's taxonomy is useful for understanding the kinds of things people are using distributed tasks to accomplish:

> ▶ **transcription and correction tasks:** inviting users to correct and/or transcribe the outputs of digitization processes;

▸ **contextualization:** adding contextual knowledge to objects, for example, by telling stories or writing articles/wiki pages with contextual data;

▸ **complementing collections:** actively pursuing additional objects to be included in a (web) exhibit or collection;

▸ **classification:** gathering descriptive metadata related to objects in a collection (social tagging is a well-known example);

▸ **co-curation:** using inspiration/expertise of nonprofessional curators to create (web) exhibits; and

▸ **crowdfunding:** collective cooperation of people who pool their money and other resources together to support efforts initiated by others.

Follow These Rules of Thumb

At my library, we've recently started to experiment with a number of crowdsourcing projects with the intent of engaging the public to help us create new research tools at the same time we are exposing our collections and promoting deeper engagement with them. As a consequence of our experiments, we have come to realize that although there is no hard, fast set of rules governing what makes a successful crowdsourcing project, there are definitely some guidelines that increase our chances for success.

First of all, **engage the user on an emotional level.** Expose the stories behind a collection, and make them relatable to users. Use feedback to create narratives (as in Old Weather, where every entry moves the ship along on a map).

Appeal to the user's better nature. We have found that participation increases dramatically when we frame our calls for participation in terms of helping the library. Frame it the same way you would any other volunteer opportunity, even if it's one that lasts only ten seconds.

Demystify the purpose. People want to participate in projects they understand. Practice your "elevator pitch" for your project: describe it in the time it takes to go ten floors in an elevator with someone. People don't get excited about typing, but they will get excited about participating in the building of an important historical research tool.

Make the task as small as possible. This one can't be stressed enough: pay extremely close attention to exactly what action you're asking people to do, and make the task as discrete as possible. If the project involves transcribing a page of text, ask participants to transcribe a sentence, or a line, or even a single word. Complicated tasks with multiple steps run the risk of ending half-complete.

Encourage continuation. Once the tasks are broken down into small enough pieces, completing one will feel like a bite-size morsel that leaves the participant wanting more. Thank the participant immediately for their contribution, and then immediately ask them to contribute a bit more.

Lower the barriers to participation. If at all possible, allow immediate and anonymous contribution. It can definitely be useful to get users to register and sign in so that you can reward top participants and track participation. But a sign-up page can be a barrier that may discourage the casual participant. A far better approach is to allow immediate participation without registration and passively communicate the benefits of signing up as the user proceeds.

Encourage a feeling of shared ownership. While critics of *Wikipedia* claim that anyone can enter false or vandalizing information, it's heartening that the converse is true: anyone can also correct and repair bad information. By allowing other users to proofread and correct what's previously been entered, you give participants a sense of pride that this is their "neighborhood" and it should be looked after.

Show results immediately. This is another critical one. When you're collecting input from participants, don't send the fruits of their labor off to some unseen holding queue; instead, post the result proudly as completed. In our What's on the Menu? project, every time a patron transcribes a dish off of a menu, the name of that dish becomes a clickable link leading to a page showing all menus where that dish appears and facts about it (earliest and latest appearances, high and low prices, etc.). If the dish was incorrectly transcribed, it can always be corrected later. For us, it was far more important to treat the contribution as official the moment it was transcribed, allowing users to see their transcription become part of the research tool instantly.

Place the project in context. Don't try to be the center of the universe; link to other reference sources. On the New York Public Library's menu project, at the moment a new dish is transcribed, a page for that dish is created that in turn contains links to canned searches on other sites from Google to MenuPages to the library catalog, encouraging immediate exploration elsewhere.

Play games. The short "participate, get feedback" cycle we're describing here lends itself extremely well to game dynamics. If possible, keep score, and give top participants some sort of public recognition.

Reward effort. If it's possible to keep track of who's participating, give rewards. Hold a special reception with refreshments in your library, and give the invitation only to online participants. If you're not tracking the identity of participants, make sure the messaging you display is loaded with gratitude.

Report results. Let users know how the project is progressing. If the goal is to transcribe a collection, show how many documents are in that collection and how many have been completed. Show progress bars to indicate how far you've come and how far there is to go. If you're using public participation to create a research tool, use a blog or social media to report how that research has been used by historians, authors, or other researchers and link to their work.

Share the fruits of labor. When content is publicly created, make the resulting product publicly available. If the goal is to create a database of some sort, make the entire database available for download, or expose data with an application programming interface (API) and encourage anyone to create mashups of your data. Promote any works that people derive from your data on your site or blog, and encourage others to do the same.

Finally, **build a community.** Getting patrons involved in a project is an ideal opportunity to unite people with a common interest around your collections. Use social networks, a blog with comments, and/or an online forum to build a conversation with the people who are your top users. Listen to feedback, take suggestions, and point out interesting findings.

Design a Project of Your Own

It's generally a bad idea to set out to do a crowdsourcing project just to do one. It's a technique for solving problems and has no inherent value—the fact that a project is crowdsourced is not a guarantee of quality. A better approach is to first look at the projects of others (either the examples provided here or others) and participate in them. Make some corrections on *Wikipedia.* Crop a few images at the Victoria & Albert Museum's website. Get a sense for what makes *you* feel proud to have participated and motivated to continue. Having done that, look at your own library and see if there are collections or tasks that would benefit from the participation of others.

Following the rules of thumb outlined earlier, pick topics and collections that you think will resonate with your patrons (whom you will want to turn into participants). Be specific. It's better to get help transcribing a single box of interesting letters, for example, than an entire archive. Items of local interest are always good, as people inherently love to learn about where they live. Topics with a broad, universal appeal are also good; at our library, we find that food and genealogy are always popular.

Be extremely clear about the task that you are trying to accomplish. Break it down into the smallest, most granular possible action, and remain relentlessly focused. Ask yourself the question, what is the least possible useful input I can get from the participant? Be honest with your answer. It's tempting to want to get much more out of the project than is reasonable. Test your interfaces with real users, and use the interfaces yourself. If you notice the least bit of difficulty completing a task, see if you can modify the design to make the process easier.

As an example, in the menu transcription project I worked on, our first prototype had users transcribing a dish, choosing a currency for the prices, entering a price, and entering the name of the section ("Entrees," "Dessert," etc.) that contained the dish. As we progressed through the prototype, we realized that the currency could be set once for the whole menu (as could whether or not the menu had prices listed at all), and the sections could be outlined later. This left the task as, "Click on a dish, and type what it says." By the end of our first month, the average visitor was transcribing over 30 dishes per visit, a testament to this reduction in awkwardness.

A good crowdsourcing task can be both explained and accomplished in seconds. It takes editing, perhaps above all, to get there.

Choose the Tools to Use

As mentioned, crowdsourcing projects cover a lot of territory. While you can certainly hire a programmer to design and build custom software for you, that's certainly not a necessity. Depending on the type of project, you can have success using simple, off-the-shelf software solutions that don't require you to do any programming of your own.

It's relatively easy to set up a **wiki** but much harder to shape and direct the community around a task. Allowing too much freedom can doom a project far more quickly than imposing too many constraints. This approach offers the most freedom and allows for serendipity and surprise in the participation you'll get.

If your main goal is to coordinate your volunteers' efforts in a more structured way than social media afford, there are online services designed specifically for this purpose. Websites such as **IdeaScale** (http://ideascale .com/) and **IdeaTorrent** (http://www.ideatorrent.org/) allow visitors to contribute ideas and then vote and comment on them to collectively assign a priority to those ideas. These tools can be especially useful at the beginning of a project, when you're faced with a number of options how to proceed. For example, if your library has hundreds of different collections that might be suitable for some sort of crowdsourcing project, you can use these idea-ranking sites to determine which ideas will resonate the most with your public.

If your project requires more constraints and more precise ways to validate input from the participants, using more specialized software is needed. There are a few websites that serve as platforms for managing online volunteering and distributed work.

One of the best known is Amazon's **Mechanical Turk** (https://www.mturk .com/mturk/welcome), a sophisticated system for managing the distribution and completion of tasks that are too subtle or complex to be completed by automated computer processes. With a bit of technical skill, you can generate tasks for completion and register them with Mechanical Turk, where users can choose to work on them. Typically, Mechanical Turk is a paid service, where you set a value for each task (prices range from less than a penny to more than $10 per completed task), but often a surprising amount of work can get completed for even a tiny amount of compensation. Mechanical Turk has been used to coordinate efforts to do everything from tagging songs by genre, to identifying types of craters on the moon, to scouring aerial photographs of the crash site of a missing airplane in the Arizona desert.

An interesting recent development is the **Sparked** (http://www.sparked .com/) microvolunteering network, which combines the distributed task creation of a Mechanical Turk with a community-oriented, nonprofit social networking angle. Sparked serves as a focal point for volunteers from around the globe who want to help worthy organizations complete discrete tasks and for the organizations that want to find volunteers.

If you have access to people with programming skills (or at least the ability to install web-based software on a server), there are a number of powerful tools available that can serve as the foundation for custom development. For text transcription efforts, the **Scripto** project (http://scripto.org/) is a very powerful, free web-based tool built on top of the MediaWiki software platform. It allows you to present scanned documents in an interface that encourages easy transcription from volunteers. Scripto is an ideal choice for handwritten or otherwise problematic texts that defy machine readability and will require a human eye and hand.

For documents where machine transcription will work but might be a bit inaccurate, make the computer do the first pass and then have your volunteers follow up and proofread, making corrections as they go. In this approach, you start by running your scanned documents and manuscripts through **optical character recognition (OCR) software**, which produces an output as a text file, a PDF document, or a more sophisticated format such as those specified by the TEI (Text Encoding Initiative) project that contain markup that more closely maps the converted text to the original scan. The resulting text can then be edited, searched, cut, pasted, and otherwise manipulated in all of the ways that plain text can be.

There are a number of software options if you need to convert a large number of scanned documents automatically, including (to name just two) **Google Tesseract** (http://code.google.com/p/tesseract-ocr/), which is a downloadable, public version of the OCR engine used by the Google Books project to turn hundreds of millions of scanned pages into searchable text; and **ABBYY FineReader** (http://www.abbyy.com/), a commercial desktop application that has emerged as one of the most accurate OCR tools available.

There are others as well, and the accuracy and power of OCR software seemingly increase every year.

The digital humanities and open source software development communities are areas of intense innovation and ongoing interest. By the time you're reading this, there are likely to be a number of innovations in applications that facilitate the management of crowdsourced projects. See "Recommended Reading" for places to keep an eye on new developments.

Build a Community around Your Project

Like many of these next-generation projects, a key component of crowdsourcing is that it is built around the cultivation of a community. Without a base of avid participants, you won't get anywhere. Getting your software launched and tested is just the start of the project; finding and maintaining that community is the core part of the job. Practical crowdsourcing has been possible only recently, and our understanding of what makes a dynamic and thriving group of volunteers is only just starting to emerge. Participants' attention can wane after they have had a certain amount of success (Bayus, 2010). See Chapter 7, "Best Practices," for a deeper look at cultivating community around your projects.

Consider the Issues of Moderation, Correction, and Approval

As covered earlier in the discussion of interactive subject guides, a common worry is that opening the door to patrons' free entry of text on a website will result in an endless stream of 14-year-olds typing nasty things that will be difficult to explain to your boss, and the project will come to a crashing halt. However, this is not usually the case at all.

First, a bit of reassurance on this front: digital vandalism is far rarer than you might expect. At this early stage of the crowdsourcing game, there is precious little statistical data to make broad generalizations about the accuracy of its output. However, most of the anecdotal evidence I have seen from both my own experiments and the case studies of others indicates that vandalism and intentional inaccuracies are very minimal.

For that matter, inaccuracies (whether the result of vandalism or human error) can go in an infinite number of directions. Accuracy, on the other hand, tends to go only in a single direction, converging on the right answer. *Wikipedia* has its share of contentious, borderline issues, but if I replace the entry for the "Classical Music" with a string of vulgarities, it's going to get cleaned up quickly because it's *clearly not right*. And in transcription tasks, a common approach (achievable with a tool like Mechanical Turk or Scripto) has become to use multiple attempts at transcribing the same manuscript from multiple users and compare them, making the transcription official only when the outputs match.

Given the tendency toward accuracy over time, a good rule of thumb is to trust your users to do the right thing first, until they give you a reason not to. I find *Wikipedia* to be one of the most inspiring projects on the web exactly because it could be wrecked in short order by malice, disinformation, or inaccuracy. But the distributed effort of thousands of volunteers keeps it up and running. The optimistic lesson therein is that most people want to do good.

Open the door to participation, make the barriers to entry as low as possible, and see if you're not surprised by the contributions you'll get.

Don't Forget the Practical and Legal Concerns

A good crowdsourcing project will generate a lot of new data or other information products. Mostly, that new output will be something you will want to share as broadly as you can. The question may come up from participating patrons whether they have any rights to that data. You need to make it very clear to people that your library owns the newly created data to do with whatever it wants and that the participants willingly relinquish any ability to restrict those rights. See Chapter 7, "Best Practices," for more details on creating a policy for patron-generated content.

▶6

MARKETING

- ▶ Set Expectations with Staff and Patrons
- ▶ Reach Your Audience Where They Are
- ▶ Use Next-Gen Tools to Document and Communicate Internally
- ▶ Encourage Use of Next-Gen Tools as a Daily Part of Librarianship
- ▶ Leverage Social Sharing Tools to Let Patrons Tell One Another about New Services
- ▶ Find Underserved Audiences

Next-generation projects like the ones described in this book inevitably center around connecting and collaborating with internal and external users. As such, getting the word out to staff and patrons is critical for success.

▶SET EXPECTATIONS WITH STAFF AND PATRONS

Here's the bad news: building an online community takes time and effort. Social sharing tools can let users find and talk with each other, but there is no magic inherent in the tools that will automatically keep an online community coherent. If you are going to commit to these types of projects, do not treat them as extra, free-time activities but as a core part of librarianship, and acknowledge them as such. It's not about getting every single staff member involved, and across-the-board mandates to force everyone to participate will likely fail. Identifying even a single staffer who is willing to answer questions, wrangle content, and make suggestions can be the key to making an online community blossom. It is far better to learn from a smaller project done well than to do a larger (and more visible) one poorly.

If your library works with volunteers, community-based online projects can be a great way to get your volunteers involved. While it's not recommended to have nonstaff members communicating out of official channels (tweeting, for instance) unsupervised on your behalf, you can still identify trusted volunteers to engage with fellow patrons in crowdsourcing projects or other interactive venues.

Aside from staff concerns, set expectations with your audience, as well. Don't give them the impression that you will be able to respond individually to every query if that's not the case. If you ask for feedback, either be prepared to respond or post a visible message that you will respond when you can.

Above all, be honest—to yourself and your management—about what you can and can't commit to. If you can't spare the staff for a given project, it's okay to say no. There are always other projects you can accomplish in the meantime. Sometimes you get lucky—you sit out the latest greatest trend for a couple of months and someone comes along and invents a new "thing" that makes implementing the old idea even easier. Projects from making a blog to viewing web analytics to putting a photo gallery online once required programming skills. Now our grandparents can do them. See Chapter 7, "Best Practices," for more ways to cultivate communities around your projects.

► REACH YOUR AUDIENCE WHERE THEY ARE

One major difference between libraries and many other kinds of cultural institutions is the nature of the relationship with the patron over time. The typical visitor to a museum, gallery, or archive is likely to visit infrequently and often is a trip planned far in advance. Both public and academic libraries, however, have patrons who visit far more frequently, with many arriving more than once a week. When reaching out to your users, bear in mind that the most important people to reach—your regular users—are already paying attention to you.

Use your metrics to see where the eyes of your patrons are likely to be focused. Your library's homepage is one obvious location, but if your library is anything like mine, the My Account pages are where users are paying the most attention. If you're launching a new web service or looking for participants in a user test, make a highlighted link or small banner ad to that effect and include inside the pages where customers log in to check their holds, fines, and so forth. The users of these pages are, by their nature, guaranteed to be at their most engaged.

Striving to be a next-generation library doesn't mean forgoing more traditional techniques, either. Use whatever works to promote awareness. For example, if your library maintains an e-mail mailing list (for a monthly newsletter or news announcements), be sure to use it to get the word out about any changes. E-mail lists have been around for a long time, but, even in the age of social media, a well-crafted e-mail message can be one of your most effective tools for getting the word out about new services. At my library, I've noticed distinct differences in the web browsing habits of users who arrive from different sources. Links from social media are great at driving first-time visitors to the site after reaching new audiences, but these visitors tend to have superficial involvement (very short visits). Blog posts tend to split the difference, with a decent mix of first-timers and regulars, leading to slightly longer visits. Visitors from our e-mail list, however, are the mirror image of social media; they are overwhelmingly regular visitors to the site (only about 20 percent new visits) but with a very deep engagement (the longest visits by time and page views of all three sources). When communicating with your regulars, e-mail is the way to go.

Finally, don't discount the value of good old print materials. When patrons are in the library, make sure that they are getting the message from physical interactions. Posters and flyers in high-visibility locations are good, but paper that can get into the hands of patrons is even better. When launching new web services, print bookmarks imprinted with the URLs and slip them into each borrowed book. And if your library prints receipts for borrowed material, see if there's an area on the receipt that can be customized with a timely message.

▶ USE NEXT-GEN TOOLS TO DOCUMENT AND COMMUNICATE INTERNALLY

The web itself was designed at the outset to be a document sharing and distribution platform and is therefore ideally suited to disseminate information about your new projects. If there is any resistance in your organization to the value of engaging deeply and publicly with social media, a great way to get your institutional foot in the door is to start with the staff.

Project management software like **Basecamp** (http://basecamphq.com/) can be a very effective way to communicate within your team. It includes threaded messages, milestones and to-dos, versioned file uploads, and user management tools. It's an especially good place to store documentation about a project if you're working with an outside vendor to do any of your software development.

The corporate social networking tool **Yammer** (http://yammer.com/) has also become very popular recently. It's based on e-mail addresses within a given domain, so if your library's e-mails end with "@mylibrary.org" and you set up a Yammer account, anyone with a "mylibrary.org" e-mail address can join your network. With elements familiar from Facebook and

Twitter, it's a great place for informal social conversation to happen among your staff.

If none of these tools appeals to your staff's taste, at least encourage the sharing of documentation and learning within your organization through some form of shared document system. Set up a wiki for internal use and see what happens. Web-based document editing tools such as Google Docs are extremely useful as well and require very little in the way of setup or special training. If your team is constantly sending Word documents back and forth to each other as e-mail attachments with names like "schedule FINAL Vers.5-Michael's edits.doc," then you can definitely benefit from a collaborative editing tool. If you or your team has never worked in an environment where documents can be edited in real time, try it. These tools are powerful yet free and are getting easier to use all of the time, and they improve communication by getting everyone looking at the same content at the same time rather than editing in turns.

► ENCOURAGE USE OF NEXT-GEN TOOLS AS A DAILY PART OF LIBRARIANSHIP

The tech staff of the giant web companies Microsoft and Google have come up with an internal process which they've given the (somewhat unfortunate) name "dogfooding." Referring to the (possibly apocryphal) story of a dog food company executive who had such faith in the quality of his product that he ate a can of it every year at the annual board meeting, it is the idea that software engineers build the best products when they use their own products themselves to solve their own problems. (Believe it or not, this inelegant phrase has its own *Wikipedia* entry: http://en.wikipedia.org/wiki/Eating_your_own_dog_food.)

It's a useful test for libraries. We talk a good game about the superiority of library materials and our original sources, but, when pressed, almost every librarian I know will admit to going straight to Google and *Wikipedia* when starting research on a question (and it's a perfectly acceptable admission). Still, the question is worth asking repeatedly: why *don't* we search our own systems first?

Encourage your librarians to use the same tools that the patrons are using. If you're trying to encourage your patrons to share via social networks or collaboratively create a research guide, make sure your staff are doing the same. Frequently, the best and most creative solutions (from music to software to films) came about because the creator was making the song or app or movie she wanted to hear, use, or see. Good solutions arise when you put yourself in the role of patron and design the best possible experience you want to have.

▶ LEVERAGE SOCIAL SHARING TOOLS TO LET PATRONS TELL ONE ANOTHER ABOUT NEW SERVICES

In Chapter 5, we stressed the importance of making sharing tools available to your patrons. Rather than just being an interesting diversion or something to do to "look cool," social media are becoming the primary way that increasing numbers of our patrons let one another know about interesting content on the web. If you do not enable them to easily share your content, you are closing off one of the most effective channels of promotion available to you (and it's largely free publicity, to boot!).

The first and most important step is to make patrons happy. In the age of Facebook, they will let others know about their experiences with your library regardless of whether those experiences are good, bad, or indifferent, so striving for the best possible experience is important. Make great stuff available and make it easy for everyone to share with people they know, and you'll find your traffic increasing.

▶ FIND UNDERSERVED AUDIENCES

When benchmarking current use, bear in mind that by definition any measure of current use will not include those who are *not* currently users of your library. If the goal of your redesign is (as is often the case) to reach new audiences, then you should take some time to try to find out as much as possible about the people in your community who are not users. Make an effort to engage them and turn them into patrons.

If at a public library, look up your community's census data. Gather from your patrons a sampling of the kind of demographic information that can be found through public census records, and make a spreadsheet that compares the percentiles of each category (age, gender, languages spoken, etc.) between your patrons and the community as a whole. Is your community older than your patrons on average? Maybe more services for seniors are in order. Are there more Chinese speakers as a percentage of your community than in your library? Perhaps it's time for more foreign language titles.

If your library is part of an academic institution, then your community is the student body and faculty. Tap the registrar's office for demographic information. How many undergrads versus graduate students are in your library? Do they have differing needs?

The pool of people who are not currently patrons is so vast that if you do not have a strategy for reaching them, you will likely not succeed. Pick a smaller subsegment of the population to target, and understand their motivations for using or not using your services. This is one place where focus groups can be a useful tool. Recruit a few people from the target audience you'd like to reach who are not current users, and ask them why they haven't considered using your library or, if they've considered it but haven't visited, why not. Their answers may be revealing: is it inconvenience that's keeping them away? Unfamiliarity with your offerings? A traumatic experience with overdue fines in the seventh grade? You might be able to find simple, easily addressed responses to their misgivings that will yield large benefits.

►7

BEST PRACTICES

- ► Cultivate Your Community
- ► Set Policies for Moderation, Community Management, and Ownership of Content
- ► Improve Constantly with Agile Methods
- ► Adhere to Standards and APIs
- ► Don't Panic

A key tenet of next-generation librarianship is to embrace the speed of technological change rather than feel threatened or frustrated by it. The fact that the world in which we operate is changing daily presents as many opportunities as challenges. Here are some basic techniques for dealing with that change.

►CULTIVATE YOUR COMMUNITY

For crowdsourcing or other community-generated projects, one of the hardest parts of the job is finding, engaging, and communicating with the people you want to turn from bystanders to audience and from audience to participants. Amassing a strong set of community-building tools is imperative for the next-generation librarian.

Blogs make an excellent starting point for the dissemination of information about your community project. Starting a blog (or a dedicated channel of your existing blog) about your project gives you a place to:

- ► explain the purpose and mission of your project and place it in context,
- ► keep your users up-to-date on the project's process,
- ► respond to frequently asked questions, and
- ► highlight interesting discoveries you or your participants find along the way.

The launch of a new crowdsourcing or community project is also an excellent chance to use the social media tools we discussed in Chapter 5 to communicate and converse with your participants. If the project is substantial enough, you can set up a Facebook fan page or Twitter account specifically for it. These platforms serve as conduits for the information about the project just as blogs do, but they have the additional benefit of being constructed around sharing so that your biggest fans also become your biggest promoters. In the age of social sharing, having passionate participants tell their friends about projects they find interesting and engaging can perform better than a professional ad campaign, with the added benefit of being well within the reach of a library-sized budget.

Twitter, Facebook, and other social media also allow you to identify particularly passionate participants and communicate with them in a very specific way. Twitter is especially effective for you to throw a shout-out to individuals; even a gesture as simple as saying "Thank you!" can go a long way toward forming an emotional connection with someone in your audience.

Blogs and social networks are also great places to tell the stories of some of the artifacts in your collection. The close attention paid to your collections via crowdsourcing projects can result in some interesting findings by your patrons. Be sure to share them with everyone, using your communications tools to both share that finding and credit the person who made the discovery. In the *Guardian* example mentioned in Chapter 5, identifying noteworthy items was the entire point. And with our historical menu project, users comment via e-mail, Facebook, and Twitter about everything from the prominence of oysters on menus in the 1900s to the impenetrably florid script on the menus of a certain hotel in Germany; such findings make for fun, interesting "retweets" and can help turn a pile of historical documents from a measurable pile of paper into a vibrant story with a context and life of its own.

► SET POLICIES FOR MODERATION, COMMUNITY MANAGEMENT, AND OWNERSHIP OF CONTENT

When giving patrons the chance to contribute their own content, the initial worries from librarians are manifold: things that reflect poorly on the library will be posted; we'll be held liable for things that are offensive or wrong; our already-stretched staff will have to spend all day cleaning up online messes left by hordes of e-vandals. However, this kind of vandalism occurs far less frequently than you might expect. After all, the Internet is very big, and your library is very small, comparatively. There are many other places to cause mayhem.

As such, if your project is starting small, the demands on your library staff to keep up with the demand for moderation may be lower than you might think. At the very least, experiment first to see what kind of response you get. It would be a shame to forgo a participatory project because of an irrational fear of imagined problems that may never actually arise.

A good solution is to put the tools for moderation in the hands of the patrons themselves and let the community police itself. The vast majority of your participants are going to have a vested interest in protecting their own efforts. Opening up your subject guide to free editing means that anyone can vandalize, but it also means that anyone can *correct* and *protect* the site. One of the beautiful things that can happen when you allow direct input from patrons is that individuals you've never met before can step up and take ownership of particular resources. For a deeper look at developing policies for collaborating with your patrons, see *Strategic Planning for Social Media in Libraries* by Sarah K. Steiner (THE TECH SET #15).

► IMPROVE CONSTANTLY WITH AGILE METHODS

It is inevitable that any software project you build or purchase will no longer meet your patrons' needs the moment it is deployed. Our libraries are not static because our patrons are not static. They are exposed to new software, new websites, new phones, tablet computers, marketing, television, advertising, and a million new inventions a month that will be invented somewhere other than your library.

If your typical web project is a long, painful process that is worked on for years and rolled out as a single, unyielding solid, then the prospect of changing needs (and tastes) on the part of your patrons can fill you with despair. No matter how you plan, no matter what percentage of the staff and patrons you've interviewed, no matter how beautiful your design, the moment you put a piece of software in front of real, live members of the public for the first time, they will inevitably surprise you. When this happens, you will have two strong urges, both of which you should resist strongly: one is to do them physical violence, and the other is to teach them the right way to do things. They are not stupid, and they are not doing it wrong. Don't get angry, and don't add instructions in hopes of clarifying; instructions are often signals of design failure. Fix the design problem.

A recent trend in software development circles is the idea of agile development. Agile methods come in many flavors, and most programmers will have their own definition of what "agile" means. But, in general, there are a few tenets that its followers adhere to (Agile Manifesto, 2012):

► Make customers happy by quickly delivering useful software.
► Welcome changing requirements, even late in development.
► Measure progress in working software.

▶ Sustain development at a constant pace instead of cramming for deadlines.

▶ Foster face-to-face, daily cooperation between business people and developers.

▶ Build projects around motivated individuals, and trust them.

▶ Pay continuous attention to technical excellence and good design.

▶ Keep things simple.

There can be a tendency in project planning to want to do everything at once in a way that necessitates immense amounts of planning up front, a lot of work in the middle, and a big-splash, all-at-once launch at the end. This is known as the "waterfall" method of project management, as the project "flows downhill" from planning to work to completion and comes out at the bottom completed. The problem with the waterfall method is that the project takes a long while to complete, and, by the time it is finished, the original requirements may have changed.

Agile methods take a different approach, breaking up big projects into smaller miniprojects. The key to agile projects is iteration, repeating the build–deploy–test–improve cycle over and over again as quickly as possible. It's a good technique to employ within libraries, which tend to be stable institutions with lots of long-term processes and lots of opportunities to evaluate impact against a fairly consistent audience. See the companion website (http://www.alatechsource.org/techset/) for more resources to learn about agile development and Chapter 8, "Metrics," for tips on evaluating your progress within each project iteration.

▶ ADHERE TO STANDARDS AND APIs

With its focus on openness, encouragement of sharing, and desire to see wide dissemination of materials, the next-generation library should be an ideal citizen of the network community. Libraries can further the cause of interoperability by adhering to open standards and building systems that expose public data in a format that can be reused and repurposed by partners and engaged members of the public.

Technical standards, from those that make up the web (HTTP, HTML5, CSS, JSON, etc.) to those that define how we store and transfer data (RDF, MARC, Dublin Core, XML, etc.) make interoperability of library systems possible. These standards have benefits both to the users of your library's data and to the maintainability of your own systems.

Application programming interfaces, or APIs, take standards a step further and define how that data can be retrieved and changed from a particular application. A key component in the growth of many of the commercial web technologies and social networks cited in this book was the fact that they offered their own APIs. Google Maps, for example, has been "mashed up" in myriad ways to track everything from crime to forest fires via a free and very flexible API. Twitter's success is in great part due to the fact that Twitter users have literally thousands of client applications besides the Twitter web interface available to them, all thanks to the free, well-documented Twitter API.

Well-documented raw data made available through a free, public API is catnip to the type of person who likes to build his own applications. These applications can frequently extend the reach of your data to unexpected places. Does your library offer an online picture collection? An API might allow someone to build an iPhone app that shows the pictures taken closest to where she's standing. Do you offer aggregate circulation data online? Someone can build an interactive chart visualizing the popularity of the top-circulated items over time.

▶ DON'T PANIC

Finally, a word of advice: There are a million things you could be doing right now to make your library better, and you're not doing them. *That is okay.* You will never be able to do every project or even to execute perfectly the projects you do choose to complete. Your goal is not to build the perfect library in one shot. It doesn't work that way.

Libraries don't get built like pieces of jewelry, with a lot of focused, intense effort producing a shiny, perfect little product. Rather, libraries grow like gardens. Your job is to water, weed, and fertilize your projects and let your garden grow at its pace.

Gardens don't have a finish line. Don't torment yourself with the question, "Why isn't my library perfect yet?" Instead, ask yourself, at the end of each day, "Did I make my patrons' experience of using the library better today, even if just a little bit?" When the answer to the latter question is "Yes," you're on the right track.

►8

METRICS

- ► **Use Web Analytics**
- ► **Plan Your Metrics Measurement Strategy Early to Avoid Mistakes**
- ► **Choose the Right Metrics to Measure**
- ► **Investigate the Analytics Software Choices**
- ► **Ask the Right Questions**

The vast amount of technological changes that are reshaping libraries can be intimidating, but not all of that change is coming from a headwind direction. Numerous tools, previously beyond the reach of most librarians, are now affordable and even free. Measurement, assessment, and statistical analysis of digital library projects are as much a part of next-generation librarianship as knowing how to set up a wiki or post on a blog.

►USE WEB ANALYTICS

For a digital librarian, the most indispensable tool in your arsenal is a solid package of web analytics. With good analytics, every visit to every page from every patron can contribute to your understanding of the way your library is being used in the networked age. Many librarians are at least passingly familiar with the top-line statistics generated by websites: page views, unique visitors, and visits. But those numbers are broad, aggregate measures, and tell, by themselves, only a small part of the narrative that makes up your web use.

The World Wide Web has become the distribution platform of choice for most digital information emanating from libraries, and, as such, good web analytics can give you insight into far more than just traffic to your main website. If your catalog is web based, analytics can help build narratives about use of your materials—and the same with online journals, your interactive research guides, and your library's intranet. Check to see if reports are being generated for each of your websites. If not, do the work to start tracking. If so, make sure that all of the decision makers and analysts on your team have access to the reports. Make sure the reports are being updated as frequently as possible.

► PLAN YOUR METRICS MEASUREMENT STRATEGY EARLY TO AVOID MISTAKES

One mistake to avoid is defining success too narrowly. A library is a complicated ecosystem composed of thousands of patron interactions, and it can be extremely difficult to predict with any precision exactly how changes in the model of service delivery will affect the total experience. With that in mind, capture as much raw data as you can. Even if you feel overwhelmed by the amount of data, make sure that a record of that data is being captured so that you can return to old records when tools improve. Web log files, which record every transaction and request for pages, sometimes contain subtleties that you don't even know you're looking for.

Another common mistake is **neglecting to set benchmarks before the start of the project**. If you don't know where you are at the beginning of the project, then you have no way of knowing how far you've come. Due to the aforementioned complexity of interactions within a library, there are very few universal scales of measurement. A university library gets 5,000 online visits a day—is that good or bad? Well, the answer depends on what the population of the student body is, how much Internet access they have, what they are studying, the holdings of the library, the design of the site, the percentage who use the physical library, and any one of hundreds of other factors. It makes a straight-up answer to the question, "Are we doing well or not?" difficult to answer.

It is a far more effective approach to **compare your own institution to itself over time** so that you can control for the vast majority of variables. If you're using quantitative measures such as visits to particular sections of the website, you need to track the existing traffic (preferably measured with the same analytics tools and methods) before undertaking improvements so you know from whence you started. If you're looking to qualitative metrics such as patron satisfaction via survey responses, have a valid survey undertaken before implementing improvements. Failing to benchmark your starting point undermines one of your strongest cases to show return on investment to the decision makers in your organization.

► CHOOSE THE RIGHT METRICS TO MEASURE

Interesting stories are almost never contained in the top-line statistics like visits and page views. Rather, these statistics are signposts indicating where the interesting stories might be hidden.

Depth-of-visit metrics, such as "pages per visit" and "time spent on site," are particularly context dependent; sometimes it's a good thing for them to go up, and sometimes it's a good thing for them to go *down*. For example, reading blogs, exploring archives, and viewing image collections are all browsing behaviors and lend themselves to longer visits as a positive outcome. Getting hours and directions, looking up daily event calendars, and checking the status of held or checkout materials are seeking behaviors, and here shorter visits are the goal. These two modes of interacting with your website are substantially different.

At my library on a given day, we see about five times as much seeking behavior as browsing behavior, so a recent web redesign saw our number of visits go up, but total page views actually dropped significantly. Had we been simply looking at "total traffic" as an unquestioned "good thing," we would have missed the real story, which is that our seekers were finding their information an average of one less page click per visit, while our browsers were staying an extra page per visit. Both outcomes were desired despite trending in opposite directions.

For libraries, a very interesting and often overlooked web metric is visitor loyalty. Do you have a good understanding of the percentage of your daily visitors who are new to your site versus those who are returning? Of those who return, how often do they return? Should you be assuming that most patrons are new to the site, or should you be offering research tools enhanced for those who might be more familiar? Libraries tend to have a solid base of loyal regulars; is your site catering to them? What is the most popular content with the regulars as opposed to the first-timers?

Constantly reevaluate the choice of metrics you are using to measure success and their context. As an example, circulation of physical materials is an important metric, but if similar materials are made available online, it may mean that circulation of those materials will drop precipitously. What may in practice be an overall increase in usage may appear as an unexplained drop in isolation.

If possible, use your analytics software to establish measurable *goals*. For example, Google Analytics allows one to define goals as a series of pages leading up to a particular page. Sample library transactions to consider tracking as goals include:

- log in to account,
- place a hold on an item or request it for delivery,
- check out a circulating item,
- place items on a list/virtual shelf,
- sign up for a mailing list, and
- subscribe to or comment on a blog.

If you are using web-based traffic analysis software (such as Google Analytics or Omniture) on your website or catalog that supports it, you can specify a series of pages leading to a goal (such as "Homepage, search page, results page, item detail page, place hold") that will allow you to see at a glance how successful particular transactions are at each step. Because these goal "funnels" are frequently used in e-commerce to track the success of online purchasing, the metrics software often allows you to assign a particular transaction an arbitrary monetary value. This can yield interesting insights even if you don't know the true monetary value of a transaction. Simply by assigning a random value—say, $1.00—to a checked-out book, these tools can determine which pages were most viewed before the transaction was completed and give a proportional share of that fictional "income" to each. At the end of the month, you can then look at the numbers and easily see which pages are contributing the most (and least!) to completed transactions. This can answer such questions as, "Are web promotions for in-library events creating checkouts?" and "Is the search box on the homepage working more effectively than the search box on the inside pages?"

▶ INVESTIGATE THE ANALYTICS SOFTWARE CHOICES

If your library does not have a go-to analytics package, there are options available ranging from simple to powerful and from free to expensive. However, this is an area where cost and performance are not necessarily proportional; website traffic analyzers have become ever more powerful in recent years, and the features of some products you can get for free today rival the most expensive offerings from just a few years ago.

There are two basic kinds of analytics software: **client-side tracking**, which uses code embedded on pages you want to track, and **server log analyzers**, which plow through the voluminous log files generated by web server software after they are created. The two varieties are not mutually exclusive, and you can use both if you wish, but usually one or the other is sufficient.

On the client side, a popular choice is Google Analytics (http://google .com/analytics), a free offering from Google. Others in this category include Mint (http://haveamint.com/), an inexpensive option that offers simplicity, and at the other end of the scale, Omniture (http://www.omniture.com/), a professional, powerful, and quite expensive option. Each requires a certain amount of setup, usually in the form of some JavaScript code that needs to be installed on your website.

There are a few drawbacks to client-side analytics, including the initial setup as well as the fact that they require JavaScript to run. Additionally, client-side tracking usually reports back to a central data storehouse on the provider's web server; your Google Analytics data, for example, is stored on Google's servers, although Google takes pains to anonymize IP addresses, so there is no individually identifiable information stored therein. This makes some libraries uneasy about using such hosted services. They also don't work as well for measuring bandwidth usage or direct downloads of binary files such as images or PDF documents, instead measuring user behavior such as clicks on particular links to those documents.

Given that the vast majority of web browsers are running JavaScript, these analytics packages work almost universally, and the advantages include excellent tracking of unique visitors and lengths of particular visits. Typically, the interfaces for exploring the statistics and generating reports are excellent. And, being hosted services, when new tools become available, they are made available to everyone.

On the server side, log file analyzers, which work by decoding information stored in your server usage logs after the fact, are perhaps a bit less powerful in parsing unique visitors but can offer much of the same insight. By the nature of their setup, you can maintain control over the whole process, because both the log files and the analyzer software live on your servers. This means you'll be responsible for their upkeep, but, if privacy issues are of paramount importance to you, they may be a better choice. They can also measure the download of any binary files, so, if you're using your analytics to track things like average page size or direct downloads of images, this is the tool you'd want.

▶ ASK THE RIGHT QUESTIONS

A solid question that can never be asked too often is, "Are you happy with the current library website?" Just ask for a straight-up approval rating, ranging from "Very dissatisfied" to "Very satisfied." **Satisfaction surveys** offer a limited amount of insight when first conducted but far more once the same survey is conducted with the same methodology a second time and the differences between one and the other are thrown into sharp relief.

Surveys can generate reliable information about the wants and needs of your patrons if you ask questions correctly, gather enough demographic data to segment your users, and ask about current use to place new services in context. Online survey tools such as SurveyMonkey (http://www.surveymonkey.com/) offer an easy way to build a survey and then gather and analyze the information through the web, avoiding the need for the printing, distribution, and after-the-fact transcription of thousands of pages of paper surveys. You can use volunteers or staff to gather information from users in person, set banners or splashes on existing websites to get feedback, e-mail links to surveys, and/or encourage patrons to go to the survey on their own.

It is worth noting that **focus groups** are generally not regarded as a source of reliable metrics, as there is no substitute for observing actual use of a system that exists in the real world. In focus groups, you're asking people what they think they'd want rather than observing their actual behavior, and that's a somewhat sketchy way to get feedback. They are notoriously susceptible to group dynamics and can also be biased by one or two strong, opinionated personalities. However, focus groups can be a useful source of generating ideas at the beginning of a project and can be useful under the right circumstances to generate ideas about services and materials that are not currently available. We've used them at my library to get insight into what we *should be* doing rather than evaluating what we *are* doing.

If your web analytics software offers it, look in your **search terms**. The things that people are searching for on your site are immensely revealing; you can approach the search box on your website as a tiny, one-question survey, with that question being, "What are you looking for right now?" Good analytics software will give you insight into both internal search terms (your search box) and external search terms (what people googled to find you). Search terms often follow a "power-law distribution," meaning that the top 5 percent of most frequently searched terms will result in a disproportionately large chunk of all searches. By looking at the top 100 or 500 search terms, examining what they lead to on your website, and making sure they're leading to the best results possible, you can get a great insight into your patrons' interests while optimizing their experience.

▶9

DEVELOPING TRENDS

- ▶ **Make Everything Mobile**
- ▶ **Delve into Augmented Reality and Location-Aware Applications**
- ▶ **Expect E-books Everywhere**
- ▶ **Watch for Continuing Innovations in the Digital Humanities**
- ▶ **Use Linked and Open Data Principles**

The question "What technological changes are on the horizon that might impact the way librarians work?" can probably be half-seriously answered "all of them!" There's a lot of change headed our way. As you look past our projects and on to the next, next generation, here are a few technologies and innovations worth keeping an eye on.

▶MAKE EVERYTHING MOBILE

We've already engaged with mobile technology earlier in this book, but that wave is still building and growing daily. Among up-and-coming technology trends, the proliferation and massive improvement of mobile devices, from smartphones to tablets and more, is the one with perhaps the greatest impact on the future direction of library service. As the distinction between "smartphones" and regular old "phones" fades and mobile Internet access gets cheaper, people will expect to use their phones to accomplish more and more tasks.

For libraries, the next wave of mobile technology will move beyond access—merely seeing the catalog on a mobile device—and move into a more seamless, interwoven experience. Patrons should be able to borrow books in any format, with and on any device, and synchronize their borrowing as they move from physical location to desktop to phone and back.

▶ DELVE INTO AUGMENTED REALITY AND LOCATION-AWARE APPLICATIONS

The proliferation of mobile devices with location awareness, spatial orientation, and cameras means that, increasingly, our patrons carry a device in their pockets with the ability to show information overlaid onto their view of a particular location. Potential library applications include showing patrons the exact location of a book, wayfinding to direct patrons to particular rooms within large libraries, and projecting annotations made by librarians and other patrons directly onto particular materials.

Scannable QR codes (see Figure 9.1) and radiofrequency ID (RFID) tags on physical materials allow a phone to identify the nearest copy of a book within the library and, better still, enable navigation by metadata within the stacks; imagine pointing your phone at a row of shelves and seeing a tag cloud appear on your phone of all of the subjects on that shelf or highlighting all of its books rated "5 stars" by your friends.

Advances in locational technology will enable interactions we can only guess at today. For more on emerging trends in location-aware library applications, see *Location-Aware Services and QR Codes for Libraries* by Joe Murphy (THE TECH SET #13).

▶ EXPECT E-BOOKS EVERYWHERE

Between the Kindle and the iPad and dozens of other user-friendly, high-quality reading devices, e-books have made their long-predicted leap to the mainstream. As libraries endeavor to keep up with the demand, new forms of interactions are being created. Web projects from WorldCat.org to Open Library.org, to HathiTrust and the Digital Public Library of America are building large-scale, shared catalogs that will increasingly direct users to

▶ Figure 9.1: Scannable QR Code

downloadable copies of e-books and other e-materials, while commercial offerings from Apple, Amazon, and every publisher are coming online and getting bigger every day. The best of these will set the standard for the quality of user experience that our patrons will expect.

▶ WATCH FOR CONTINUING INNOVATIONS IN THE DIGITAL HUMANITIES

We've reached a point on the curve of computing progress that one new Apple iPad tablet has more computing power than a Cray supercomputer, the fastest computer in the world in 1985 (Markoff, 2011). Given the ever-increasing amount of spare processing cycles in the world, it was inevitable that supercomputer-sized power could be brought to bear on questions not previously thought of as technologically analyzable. A growing number of technologists have increasingly begun to analyze literature, history, geography, fine arts, and other fields in the humanities with computational tools and methodological rigor previously reserved for the sciences.

Whether it's analyzing the entire corpus of Google Books to trace occurrences of a single word throughout written history, transposing decades of handwritten census data onto zoomable maps, or sorting the complete works of Picasso by shape and color, the new and growing field of Digital Humanities is developing new forms of scholarship. As library collections become increasingly digital, taxonomized, tagged, and hyperlinked, libraries themselves are poised to be key players in their development and growth, offering both the expertise of its staff in navigating large digital collections and the extraordinarily valuable resource that is the collections themselves.

▶ USE LINKED AND OPEN DATA PRINCIPLES

Linked data, a term coined by World Wide Web inventor Tim Berners-Lee in 2006, is the method of publishing structured data on the web to facilitate its use, reuse, and interconnectivity with other platforms. While certain specifications of linked data such as RDF/XML are becoming approved standards through the same organizations that govern the rules of the web, there are other efforts along similar lines being proposed independently. In 2011, the first summit for Linked and Open Data for Libraries, Archives, and Museums brought together practitioners from across the digital cultural community to discuss ways in which their collections can be exposed and used. (Check out the conference website and proceedings at http://lod-lam .net/summit/.) Recent developments like Schema.org, a partnership among major search engine companies to promote standardized markup of certain types of data within HTML pages, are promoting linked data principles in everyday use (e.g., Google recently launched a recipe search engine, and, by using a Google-approved recipe schema, any recipes on your website can automatically be included and sorted, not just by keyword, but by ingredient, cooking time, etc.).

As the machines connected to the edges of the Internet grow ever more sophisticated, expect the need for more intelligent description of content flowing across it to increase. For more on new trends in structured data and the Semantic Web, see *Semantic Web Technologies and Social Searching for Librarians* by Robin M. Fay and Michael P. Sauers (THE TECH SET #20).

RECOMMENDED READING

It should go without saying that working in a field where changes in technology today can have such a massive impact on the choices you will need to make tomorrow morning, it is imperative to stay informed. Fortunately, in today's interconnected world, staying informed is easier than ever. In fact, the more necessary skill is filtering out the relevant materials from an almost endless selection.

BLOGS AND WIKIS

There are literally thousands of great blogs of interest to the library technologist. Here are just a few of my consistent favorites. Pro tip: Use an RSS reader such as Google Reader (web-based) or NetNewsWire (desktop application) if you don't already!

- Stephen Abram, *Stephen's Lighthouse* (http://stephenslighthouse.com/). Frequent posts on library industry and strategy.
- Sarah Houghton-Jan, *Librarian in Black* (http://librarianinblack.net). Quirky, essential advice from the librarian's perspective.
- *LibSuccess Best Practices Wiki* (http://www.libsuccess.org/). An extensive wiki covering best practices in all manner of library practice, digital and otherwise.
- Nieman Journalism Lab (http://www.niemanlab.org/). Perhaps a bit more of a news service than a blog but required reading either way.
- Nina Simon, *Museum 2.0* (http://museumtwo.blogspot.com/). A museum technologist, Nina's insights into patron engagement nonetheless have massive usefulness to the library crowd.
- Mike Shatzkin, *The Shatzkin Files* (http://www.idealog.com/blog). Insights into the business side of publishing from a nearly 50-year veteran of the publishing industry.

► David Weinberger, *Joho the Blog* (http://www.hyperorg.com/blogger/). One of the principals of the Harvard Library Innovation Lab and coauthor of *The Cluetrain Manifesto* (Basic Books, 2001).

►BOOKS

I find the web to be a better source of information about rapidly changing technology, so my taste in books tends to run to timeless advice on design, usability, and customer service.

► Nick Bilton, *I Live in the Future and Here's How It Works* (Crown Business, 2010). How technology is changing everyday work and life.
► Robert Darnton, *The Case for Books* (Public Affairs, 2009). Meditations on the past, present, and future of books from the director of Harvard University Library.
► Kevin Kelly, *What Technology Wants* (Viking, 2010). Very long-term thinking about how technology evolves and the degree to which change is inevitable.
► Donald Norman, *The Design of Everyday Things* (Doubleday Business, 1990). A great primer on the relationship between emotional states and usability.
► Clay Shirky, *Here Comes Everybody* (Penguin Group, 2008). Insight into the ways that the massive interconnectedness afforded by the web is changing the way people interact with institutions and each other.
► Edward Tufte, *Envisioning Information* (Graphics Press, 1990). Perhaps the single best book ever written on the visual design of information-bearing materials.
► Paco Underhill, *Why We Buy: The Science of Shopping* (Simon & Schuster, 2000). Essential reading for understanding the psychology of retail interactions, with great implications for the library world.

►PEOPLE TO FOLLOW ON TWITTER

Twitter is an excellent source of timely professional information. There's something about the format that makes it very amenable to sharing developments in the library and web technology worlds. Here is a small sample of the library/museum/digital humanities people I follow.

► Tim Carmody (@tcarmody), technology writer and "bookfuturist."
► Nicole Engard (@nengard), specialist in open source software for libraries.

▶ Amanda French (@amandafrench), digital humanities scholar.

▶ Jose Afonso Furtado (@jafurtado), library director and prolific tweeter of great links.

▶ Effie Kapsalis (@digitaleffie), head of New Media at the Smithsonian.

▶ James Neal (@james3neal), another prolific tweeter of interesting links, currently at the Maryland Institute for Technology in the Humanities (MITH).

▶ Bethany Nowviskie (@nowviskie), director of digital research at University of Virginia.

▶ Trevor Owens (@tjowens), archivist at the Library of Congress and creator of crowdsourcing software.

▶ Pew Internet & American Life Project (@pewinternet), so you can know the moment they put out one of their great reports.

▶ Nancy Proctor (@nancyproctor), specialist in mobile technology for the Smithsonian.

▶ Tom Scheinfeldt (@foundhistory), director of the Center for History and New Media.

▶CONFERENCES

Aside from the big ones you might be familiar with, such as American Library Association (ALA), Digital Library Forum (DLF), Coalition for Networked Information (CNI), and Computers in Libraries, here are a few that might not be on your radar.

▶ THATCamp (http://thatcamp.org/), or "the Humanities and Technology Camp," an "unconference"-style informal get-together that has spawned offshoots in numerous cities and countries.

▶ M-Libraries (http://www.libsuccess.org/index.php?title=M-Libraries), a biennial conference addressing the state of mobile technology in libraries.

▶ International Linked Open Data in Libraries, Archives, and Museums Summit (LOD-LAM) (http://lod-lam.net/summit/), a June 2011 convention of experts from the humanities and sciences to catalyze practical, actionable approaches to publishing Linked Open Data.

If you use Twitter, the website Lanyrd (http://lanyrd.com/) is a tool that ties into your Twitter feed and points out conferences that people in your feed are speaking at, attending, or are interested in attending. If you're allowed only a limited number of conferences a year to attend, then Lanyrd can help you choose the ones attended by the most interesting and relevant people you follow.

► SEE MORE

I'm certain I left many, many great resources out (apologies in advance to those who know who you are). See the companion website (http://www.ala techsource.org/techset/) for an expanded list.

REFERENCES

Agile Manifesto. 2012. "Principles Behind the Agile Manifesto." AgileManifesto.org. Accessed February 6. http://agilemanifesto.org/principles.html.

Anderson, J., and L. Rainie. 2010. "The Future of Social Relations." Pew Internet and American Life Project. http://pewinternet.org/Reports/2010/The-future-of-social-relations/Overview.aspx.

Andersen, M.. 2009. "Four Crowdsourcing Lessons from the Guardian's (Spectacular) Expenses-Scandal Experiment." *Nieman Journalism Lab*, June 23. http://www.niemanlab.org/2009/06/four-crowdsourcing-lessons-from-the-guardians-spectacular-expenses-scandal-experiment/.

Anderson, N. 2007. "Experts Rate Wikipedia's Accuracy Higher Than Non-experts." Condé Nast Digital. http://arstechnica.com/old/content/2006/11/8296.ars.

Apple Corporation. 2010. "iTunes Store Tops 10 Billion Songs Sold." Retrieved from http://www.apple.com/pr/library/2010/02/25iTunes-Store-Tops-10-Billion-Songs-Sold.html.

Bayus, Barry L. 2010. "Crowdsourcing and Individual Creativity Over Time: The Detrimental Effects of Past Success." Social Science Research Network. SSRN: http://ssrn.com/abstract=1667101.

Berners-Lee, Tim. 2006. "Linked Data." W3.org Design Issues. http://www.w3.org/DesignIssues/LinkedData.html.

Christensen, Clayton M. 2003. *The Innovator's Dilemma: The Revolutionary Book That Will Change the Way You Do Business.* New York: HarperPaperbacks.

Dalbello, M. 2004. "Institutional Shaping of Cultural Memory: Digital Library as Environment for Textual Transmission." *The Library Quarterly*, 74, no. 3: 265–298.

Doctorow, Cory. 2006. "Disney Exec: Piracy Is Just a Business Model." *BoingBoing* (blog), October 10. http://boingboing.net/2006/10/10/disney-exec-piracy-i.html.

Ganster, L., and B. Schumacher. 2009. "Expanding Beyond Our Library Walls: Building an Active Online Community through Facebook." *Journal of Web Librarianship*, 3, no. 2: 111–128.

Gardner, Sue. 2010. "From Wikimedia Executive Director Sue Gardner." Wikimedia Foundation. http://wikimediafoundation.org/wiki/WMFSG011/en/US.

Giles, Jim. 2005. "Internet Encyclopaedias Go Head to Head," *Nature*, 438: 900–901. Retrieved from http://www.nature.com/nature/journal/v438/n7070/full/438900a.html.

Kingma, B. 2010. "The Economics of Libraries, Cost-Benefit Analysis, and Return on Investment." ARL Lib-Value: Return on Investment (ROI) for Academic Libraries Workshop, Washington, DC.

Lavoie, B. 2011. "The Top 25 US Public Libraries' Collective Collection, as Represented in WorldCat." OCLC Research. http://www.oclc.org/research/publications/library/2011/lavoie-ndpl.pdf.

Llewellyn, C. 2011. *Know the Past, Find the Future: The New York Public Library at 100.* New York: Penguin Classics, pp. 99–100.

Markoff, John. 2011. "The iPad in Your Hand: As Fast as a Supercomputer of Yore." *The New York Times* (blog), May 9. http://bits.blogs.nytimes.com/2011/05/09/the-ipad-in-your-hand-as-fast-as-a-supercomputer-of-yore/?scp=1&sq=The%20iPad%20in%20Your%20Hand:%20As%20Fast%20as%20a%20Supercomputer%20of%20Yore&st=cse.

Newell, T. 2004. "Representing Library Users and Professionals on Websites: A Visual Grammar Approach for Library Image-Makers and Library Educators." *Journal of Education for Library and Information Science*, 45, no. 4: 307–316.

Oomen, Johan, and Lora Arroyo. 2011. "Crowdsourcing in the Cultural Heritage Domain: Opportunities and Challenges." Crowdsourcing LLC. http://www.crowdsourcing.org/document/crowdsourcing-in-the-cultural-heritage-domain-opportunities-and-challenges/4555.

Parr, Ben. 2011. "EXCLUSIVE: Google to Retire Blogger and Picasa Brands in Google+ Push." Mashable, Inc. http://mashable.com/2011/07/05/google-blogger-picasa-rebranding/.

Polansky, Adam. 2007. "Faceted Feature Analysis: How to Use Bias to Get Unbiased Project Scope." *Boxes and Arrows*, July 7. http://www.boxesandarrows.com/view/faceted-feature.

Powazek, Derek. 2009. "Spammers, Evildoers and Opportunists." *Powazek* (blog), October 12. http://powazek.com/posts/2090.

Rodger, E. J., C. Jörgensen, and G. D'Elia. 2005. "Partnerships and Collaboration among Public Libraries, Public Broadcast Media, and Museums: Current Context and Future Potential." *The Library Quarterly*, 75, no. 1: pp. 42–66.

Sharma, Sunita. 2010. "Public's Wishes Revealed." MLA: Museums, Libraries, and Archives, November 22. http://www.mla.gov.uk/news_and_views/press_releases/2010/ipsosmori.

Shirky, Clay. 2009. "How Social Media Can Make History." TED Talks presentation. http://www.ted.com/talks/clay_shirky_how_cellphones_twitter_facebook_can_make_history.html.

Springshare. 2011. "Guide FAQ." Springshare. Accessed June 20. http://guidefaq .com/a.php?qid=7360.

Sun Microsystems. 1999. "Code Conventions for the Java Programming Language." Sun Microsystems, Inc. http://java.sun.com/docs/codeconv/html/Code Conventions.doc.html#16712.

Tenopir, C., A. Love, J. Park, L. Wu, A. Baer, and R. Mays. 2010. "University Investment in the Library, Phase II: An International Study of the Library's Value to the Grants Process." Library Connect White Paper #2, Elsevier.

Underhill, Paco. 2000. *Why We Buy: The Science of Shopping*. New York: Simon and Schuster.

Wikimedia Foundation. 2010. "Fundraising 2010." Wikimedia Foundation. http:// meta.wikimedia.org/wiki/Fundraising_2010.

Wikimedia Foundation. 2011. "Wikipedia:About." Wikimedia Foundation. Accessed May 27. http://en.wikipedia.org/wiki/Wikipedia:About.

Wikipedia. 2011. "Joy's Law (management)." Wikimedia Foundation. Accessed May 27. http://en.wikipedia.org/wiki/Joy's_Law_(management).

Wilhelm, Alex. 2010. "How Many Kindles Have Been Sold?" The Next Web, July 29. http://thenextweb.com/us/2010/07/29/how-many-kindles-have-been-sold/.

YouTube. 2010. "A 2.5 Year-Old Has a First Encounter with an iPad." YouTube. http://www.youtube.com/watch?v=pT4EbM7dCMs on 2011-05-27.

Zeldman, Jeffrey, and Ethan Marcotte. 2010. *Designing with Web Standards*. Indianapolis, IN: New Riders.

INDEX

Page numbers followed by the letter "f" indicate figures.

ABOUT THE AUTHOR

Michael Lascarides is the Senior Manager for Web Initiatives for the New York Public Library, where he oversees the developers and designers responsible for creating many of the library's numerous web-based projects. Michael is a frequent speaker at library and web conferences in the United States and abroad. Prior to joining NYPL in 2008, he worked as a web programmer, designer, and information architect for a wide variety of commercial clients. He teaches in the MFA Computer Art program at the School of Visual Arts and holds a BS in Information Systems Management from New York University.

CPSIA information can be obtained at www.ICGtesting.com
Printed in the USA
LVOW130840290113

317676LV00003B/312/P

9 781555 707873